CAMBRIDGE

CB126766

AMERICAN EMPOWER

STUDENT'S BOOK B
WITH DIGITAL PACK

A1
STARTER

Adrian Doff, Craig Thaine
Herbert Puchta, Jeff Stranks, Peter Lewis-Jones
with Rachel Godfrey

CAMBRIDGE

AMERICAN EMPOWER is a six-level general English course for adult and young adult learners, taking students from beginner to advanced level (CEFR A1 to C1). *American Empower* combines course content from Cambridge University Press with validated assessment from the experts at Cambridge Assessment English.

American Empower's unique mix of engaging classroom materials and reliable assessment enables learners to make consistent and measurable progress.

Content you'll love.

Assessment you can trust.

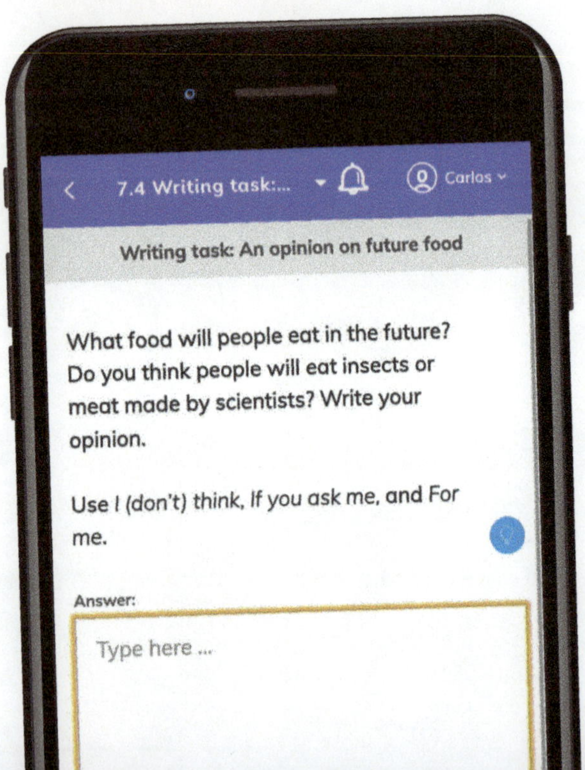

Better Learning with *American Empower*

Better Learning is our simple approach where **insights** we've gained from research have helped shape **content** that drives **results**.

Learner engagement

1 Content that informs and motivates

Insights
Sustained motivation is key to successful language learning and skills development.

Content
Clear learning goals, thought-provoking images, texts, and speaking activities, plus video content to arouse curiosity.

Results
Content that surprises, entertains, and provokes an emotional response, helping teachers to deliver motivating and memorable lessons.

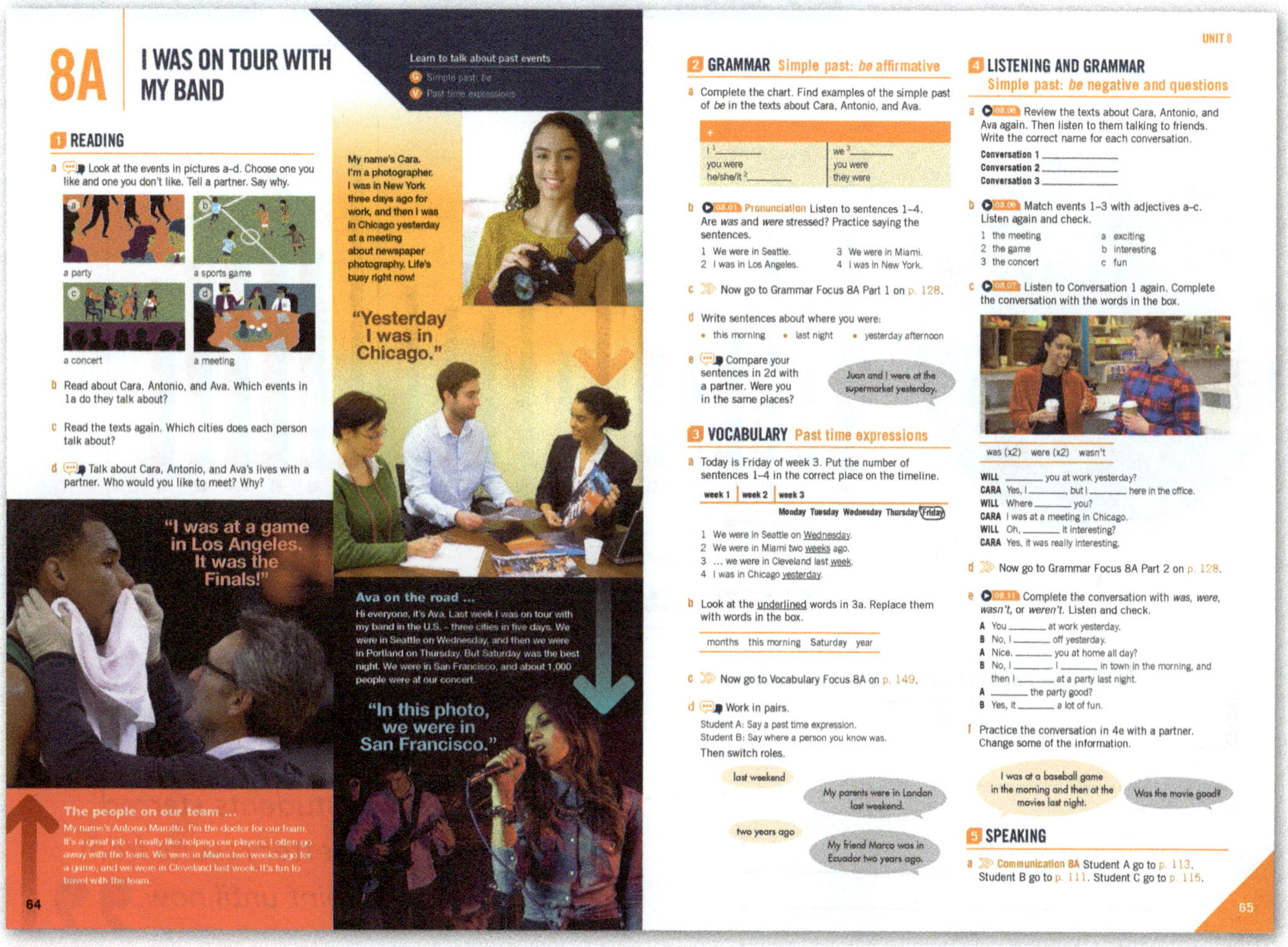

8A I WAS ON TOUR WITH MY BAND

Learn to talk about past events
G Simple past: *be*
V Past time expressions

1 READING

a Look at the events in pictures a–d. Choose one you like and one you don't like. Tell a partner. Say why.

a a party b a sports game c a concert d a meeting

b Read about Cara, Antonio, and Ava. Which events in 1a do they talk about?

c Read the texts again. Which cities does each person talk about?

d Talk about Cara, Antonio, and Ava's lives with a partner. Who would you like to meet? Why?

My name's Cara. I'm a photographer. I was in New York three days ago for work, and then I was in Chicago yesterday at a meeting about newspaper photography. Life's busy right now!

"Yesterday I was in Chicago."

"I was at a game in Los Angeles. It was the Finals!"

The people on our team ...
My name's Antonio Marotto. I'm the doctor for our team. It's a great job – I really like helping our players. I often go away with the team. We were in Miami two weeks ago for a game, and we were in Cleveland last week. It's fun to travel with the team.

Ava on the road ...
Hi everyone, it's Ava. Last week I was on tour with my band in the U.S. – three cities in five days. We were in Seattle on Wednesday, and then we were in Portland on Thursday. But Saturday was the best night. We were in San Francisco, and about 1,000 people were at our concert.

"In this photo, we were in San Francisco."

64

UNIT 8

2 GRAMMAR Simple past: *be* affirmative

a Complete the chart. Find examples of the simple past of *be* in the texts about Cara, Antonio, and Ava.

+	
I [1] ______	we [3] ______
you were	you were
he/she/it [2] ______	they were

b 08.01 Pronunciation Listen to sentences 1–4. Are *was* and *were* stressed? Practice saying the sentences.

1 We were in Seattle. 2 I was in Los Angeles. 3 We were in Miami. 4 I was in New York.

c Now go to Grammar Focus 8A Part 1 on p. 128.

d Write sentences about where you were:
- this morning
- last night
- yesterday afternoon

e Compare your sentences in 2d with a partner. Were you in the same places?

Juan and I were at the supermarket yesterday.

3 VOCABULARY Past time expressions

a Today is Friday of week 3. Put the number of sentences 1–4 in the correct place on the timeline.

week 1 | week 2 | week 3
Monday Tuesday Wednesday Thursday Friday

1 We were in Seattle on Wednesday.
2 We were in Miami two weeks ago.
3 ... we were in Cleveland last week.
4 I was in Chicago yesterday.

b Look at the underlined words in 3a. Replace them with words in the box.

months this morning Saturday year

c Now go to Vocabulary Focus 8A on p. 149.

d Work in pairs.
Student A: Say a past time expression.
Student B: Say where a person you know was.
Then switch roles.

last weekend — My parents were in London last weekend.
two years ago — My friend Marco was in Ecuador two years ago.

4 LISTENING AND GRAMMAR Simple past: *be* negative and questions

a Review the texts about Cara, Antonio, and Ava again. Then listen to them talking to friends. Write the correct name for each conversation.

Conversation 1 ______
Conversation 2 ______
Conversation 3 ______

b Match events 1–3 with adjectives a–c. Listen again and check.

1 the meeting a exciting
2 the game b interesting
3 the concert c fun

c 08.07 Listen to Conversation 1 again. Complete the conversation with the words in the box.

was (x2) were (x2) wasn't

WILL ______ you at work yesterday?
CARA Yes, I ______, but I ______ here in the office.
WILL Where ______ you?
CARA I was at a meeting in Chicago.
WILL Oh, ______ it interesting?
CARA Yes, it was really interesting.

d Now go to Grammar Focus 8A Part 2 on p. 128.

e 08.11 Complete the conversation with *was*, *were*, *wasn't*, or *weren't*. Listen and check.

A You ______ at work yesterday.
B No, I ______ off yesterday.
A Nice. ______ you at home all day?
B No, I ______. I ______ in town in the morning, and then I ______ at a party last night.
A ______ the party good?
B Yes, it ______ a lot of fun.

f Practice the conversation in 4e with a partner. Change some of the information.

I was at a baseball game in the morning and then at the movies last night. — Was the movie good?

5 SPEAKING

a Communication 8A Student A go to p. 113. Student B go to p. 111. Student C go to p. 115.

65

2 Personalized and relevant

Insights
Language learners benefit from frequent opportunities to personalize their responses.

Content
Personalization tasks in every unit make the target language more meaningful to the individual learner.

Results
Personal responses make learning more memorable and inclusive, with all students participating in spontaneous spoken interaction.

> "There are so many adjectives to describe such a wonderful series, but in my opinion it's very reliable, practical, and modern."

Zenaide Brianez, Director of Studies, Instituto da Língua Inglesa, Brazil

Measurable progress

1 Assessment you can trust

Insights
Tests developed and validated by Cambridge Assessment English, the world leaders in language assessment, to ensure they are accurate and meaningful.

Content
End-of-unit tests, mid- and end-of-course competency tests, and personalized CEFR test report forms provide reliable information on progress with language skills.

Results
Teachers can see learners' progress at a glance, and learners can see measurable progress, which leads to greater motivation.

Results of an impact study showing % improvement of Reading levels, based on global *Empower* students' scores over one year.

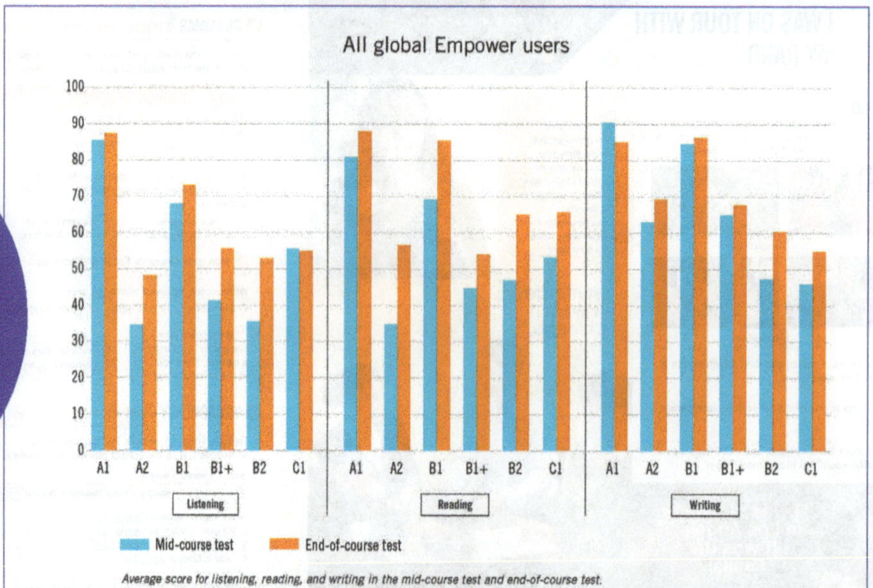

Average score for listening, reading, and writing in the mid-course test and end-of-course test. Based on global students' scores from August 2016 to July 2017.

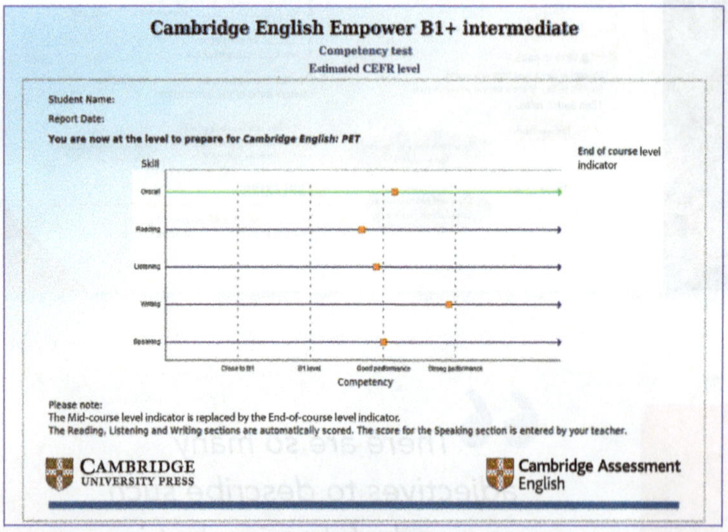

> *We started using the tests provided with Empower and our students started showing better results from this point until now.*

Kristina Ivanova, Director of Foreign Language Training Centre, ITMO University, Saint Petersburg, Russia

2 Evidence of impact

Insights
Schools and colleges need to show that they are evaluating the effectiveness of their language programs.

Content
Empower (British English) impact studies have been carried out in various countries, including Russia, Brazil, Turkey, and the UK, to provide evidence of positive impact and progress.

Results
Colleges and universities have demonstrated a significant improvement in language level between the mid- and end-of-course tests, as well as a high level of teacher satisfaction with *Empower*.

Manageable learning

1 Mobile friendly

Insights
Learners expect online content to be mobile friendly but also flexible and easy to use on any digital device.

Content
American Empower provides easy access to Digital Workbook content that works on any device and includes practice activities with audio.

Results
Digital Workbook content is easy to access anywhere, and produces meaningful and actionable data so teachers can track their students' progress and adapt their lesson accordingly.

"I had been studying English for 10 years before university, and I didn't succeed. But now with Empower *I know my level of English has changed."*

Nikita, *Empower* Student, ITMO University, Saint Petersburg, Russia

2 Corpus-informed

Insights
Corpora can provide valuable information about the language items learners are able to learn successfully at each CEFR level.

Content
Two powerful resources – Cambridge Corpus and English Profile – informed the development of the *Empower* course syllabus and the writing of the materials.

Results
Learners are presented with the target language they are able to incorporate and use at the right point in their learning journey. They are not overwhelmed with unrealistic learning expectations.

Rich in practice

1 Language in use

Insights
It is essential that learners are offered frequent and manageable opportunities to practice the language they have been focusing on.

Content
Throughout the *American Empower* Student's Book, learners are offered a wide variety of practice activities, plenty of controlled practice, and frequent opportunities for communicative spoken practice.

Results
Meaningful practice makes new language more memorable and leads to more efficient progress in language acquisition.

8B HE SAW A BEAR

Learn to describe events in the past
- Simple past: affirmative
- Free time activities

1 READING

a Look at pictures 1–3 below. Match the pictures to the animal names. Where do they usually live? What do you know about them?
___ deer ___ bear ___ hippo

b Read the stories below. Write the story titles next to the sentences.
1 Hippos were on a rugby field. ___
2 Three deer were in a woman's apartment. ___
3 A bear was in a man's backyard. ___

c Read the stories again. Complete the information.

	Where?	When?	Animal activity?
Andrew from Utah	at home		
Ben from South Africa		evening	
A woman from Indiana			jump

d Talk about the questions.
1 Which story do you like?
2 Which animals sometimes come into houses in your country?
3 What do you do if a wild animal comes to your house?

WILD STORIES!

CURIOUS CREATURE
Andrew Singer from Utah was at home in his house on a farm. One evening he was in the kitchen, and he heard something strange in the backyard, so he looked out the window. He saw a bear in the backyard. The bear walked around the backyard and looked in the windows of the house. It tried to open the kitchen door, and the man was really scared. It wasn't possible for the bear to get in, so it went away. The man thinks the bear was hungry, but it's not a good idea to give bears food.

SURPRISE VISITORS
A woman from Indiana had an apartment with a yard. In the evening, she went into her living room and watched TV. She heard something in her bedroom, so she went to look. She saw three deer near her bed. They came into the living room and jumped on her sofa, then they went into the bathroom. The woman called 911, and the police came to catch the deer. She had an exciting night with her three new friends!

READY TO PLAY
Ben Kruger from South Africa loves playing rugby. He has a business in Limpopo, a city in the north of South Africa. One night after work, he went to a rugby field nearby. It was dark, and he saw something on the field. It was large, but it wasn't a person – it was a hippopotamus (hippo)! Then he saw another hippo and then another – there were a lot of them. The hippos ate some grass and then went away. Ben thinks the hippos were from a river near the rugby field.

66

UNIT 8

2 GRAMMAR Simple past: affirmative

a Read the stories again and find the simple past forms of the verbs in the chart. Listen and check.

A Verb	A Past form	B Verb	B Past form
look	looked	have	had
watch		hear	
call		eat	
jump		see	
walk		go	
try		come	

b Answer the questions about the chart in 2a.
1 What do we add to the verbs in A to make the past form?
2 Do the verbs in B all change in the same way or in different ways?

c Sound and spelling /t/ and /d/

d Cover the chart in 2a. Test a partner.
Student A: Say a verb.
Student B: Say the past form.
Then switch roles.

e Now go to Grammar Focus 8B on p. 128.

f Complete the sentences so they are true for you.
1 Yesterday I called ___ (a person)
2 Last month I saw ___ (a TV show)
3 Last weekend I went to ___ (a place)
4 Last night I ate ___ (food)
Tell your partner about your sentences.

3 LISTENING AND VOCABULARY Free time activities

a Listen to three conversations about the three stories. In each conversation, some information is incorrect. What is the wrong information?

b Listen to the sentences from the conversations. Use the correct verb in the box.

read (x2) talked went had watched heard

c Match verbs 1 to 6 with a word or phrase in the box to make more simple past phrases.

d Listen to Emily talk about the things she did yesterday. Put pictures a–e in the correct order.

e Complete what Emily says with phrases from 3c. Then listen again and check.

f Now go to Vocabulary Focus 8B on p. 160.

g Complete the sentences about free time activities.
1 When I was a child, I ___
2 After work / school, I often ___
3 On weekends, I like to ___

h Tell other students your sentences in 3g. What free time activities were/are popular ... ?

4 SPEAKING

a Communication 8B Student A go to p. 113. Student B go to p. 111.

67

2 Beyond the classroom

> *There are plenty of opportunities for personalization.*

Elena Pro, Teacher, EOI de San Fernando de Henares, Spain

Insights
Progress with language learning often requires work outside of the classroom, and different teaching models require different approaches.

Content
American Empower is available with a print workbook, online practice, documentary-style videos that expose learners to real-world English, plus additional resources with extra ideas and fun activities.

Results
This choice of additional resources helps teachers to find the most effective ways to motivate their students both inside and outside the classroom.

Unit overview

Unit Opener

Getting started page – Clear learning objectives to give an immediate sense of purpose.

Lessons A and B

Grammar and Vocabulary – Input and practice of core grammar and vocabulary, plus a mix of skills.

Digital Workbook (online, mobile): Grammar and Vocabulary.

Lesson C

Everyday English – Functional language in common, everyday situations.

Digital Workbook (online, mobile): Listening, Speaking, Reading, and Writing

Unit Progress Test

Review

Extra practice of grammar, vocabulary, and pronunciation. Also a "Review your progress" section for students to reflect on the unit.

Mid- / End-of-course test

Additional practice

Further practice is available for outside of the class with these components.

Digital Workbook (online, mobile)

Workbook (printed)

Components

Resources – Available on cambridgeone.org

- Audio
- Video
- Unit Progress Tests (Print)
- Unit Progress Tests (Online)
- Mid- and end-of-course assessment (Print)
- Mid- and end-of-course assessment (Online)
- Digital Workbook (Online)
- Photocopiable Grammar, Vocabulary, and Pronunciation worksheets

This page is intentionally left blank.

This page is intentionally left blank.

CONTENTS

CLASSROOM LANGUAGE

00.02 Listen and read.

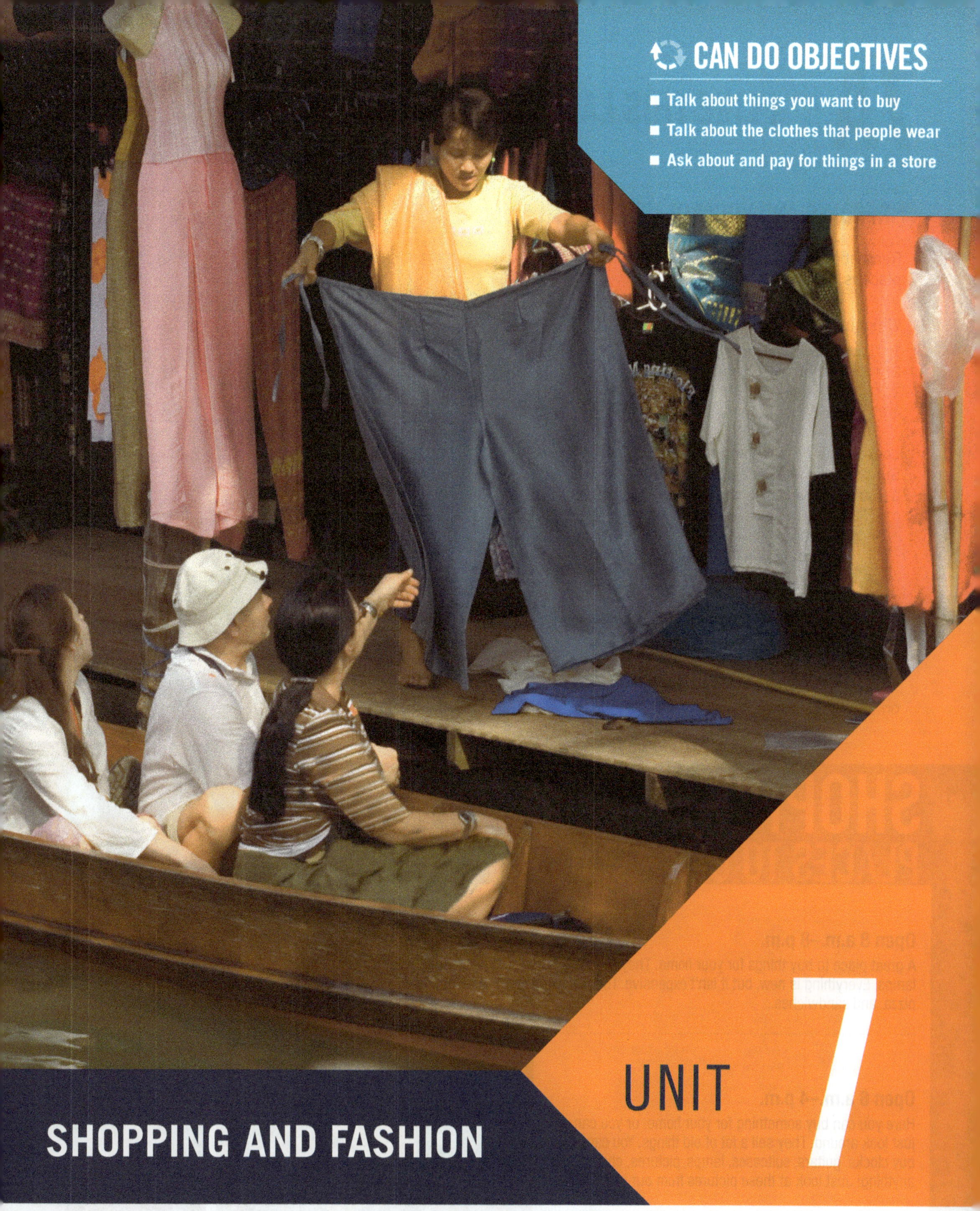

CAN DO OBJECTIVES

- Talk about things you want to buy
- Talk about the clothes that people wear
- Ask about and pay for things in a store

UNIT 7

SHOPPING AND FASHION

GETTING STARTED

a Look at the picture and answer the questions.

1 Are the people in the boat … ?
- ☐ on vacation
- ☐ shopping for food
- ☐ shopping for clothes
- ☐ friends
- ☐ family

2 What question does the woman in the boat ask?
3 What clothes can you see in the picture?

b Talk about the questions.

1 What do you like to buy when you go shopping?
2 What clothes do you have?
3 What color clothes do you like?

7A I LIKE THIS LAMP

Learn to talk about things you want to buy

G *this, that, these, those*

V Common objects 2; Prices

1 READING AND VOCABULARY Common objects 2

a Read about three places to shop. Which place is in the pictures?

b Which place is good for these people?

1 "I want a new bed for my apartment."
2 "I love old books and magazines."
3 "I always finish work at 7:00 p.m."
4 "I think old lamps are beautiful."

c Look at the pictures and read about The Sunday Flea Market again. Match the objects a–f with the words in the box.

suitcase lamp clock guitar picture chair

d Talk with other students about which object you would like to buy in the pictures. Say why. Which object do most people want?

e Now go to Vocabulary Focus 7A on p. 147.

f **Sound and spelling** /b/, /p/, /g/, and /k/

1 Complete the words in the chart. They are all common objects.

Sound 1 /b/	Sound 2 /p/	Sound 3 /g/	Sound 4 /k/
__ag __all	__lant __late __icture	__lass __uitar	__up suit__ase __lo__ __

2 07.02 Listen and check.
3 Which sound is spelled in different ways in the chart?
4 Practice saying the words.

g Work in pairs.

Student A: You have a stall at the flea market. Write five things you sell. Don't show Student B.
Student B: What does Student A sell?

Do you sell guitars?
No, sorry.
Do you have glasses?
Yes, I do. Here you go.

SHOPPING
PLACES TO GO

MEGA HOME STORE

Open 8 a.m.–8 p.m.

A great place to buy things for your home. They sell beds, pillows, tables, chairs, and lamps. Everything is new, but it isn't expensive. There's also a good café with drinks, pizza, and sandwiches.

THE SUNDAY FLEA MARKET

Open 6 a.m.–4 p.m.

Here you can buy something for your home, or you can just look around. They sell a lot of old things. You can buy clocks, guitars, suitcases, lamps, pictures, chairs … anything! Just look at these pictures from our readers!

BOOKS & CO.

Open 9 a.m.–6 p.m.

A very interesting bookstore. They sell old and new books, and they also have magazines, pictures, old photographs, and music. If you like old books and pictures, this is the place for you.

2 LISTENING AND GRAMMAR
this, that, these, those

a 07.03 Kate and Edward are at Mega Home Store. Listen to their conversation and answer the questions.

1 Who likes the plant and the chairs?
2 Who likes the phone, Kate or Edward?
3 How much is the speaker?
4 Does Kate think it's a good price?

b 07.04 Listen to Kate and Edward. Complete the sentences with *this*, *that*, *these*, or *those*.

1 "I like ________ plant. What do you think?"
2 "Or ________ chairs. They're really nice."
3 "Oh, look. ________ plates are beautiful."
4 "Look at ________ speaker. That's so cool."

c Complete the chart with the words in 2b.

Singular	this	
Plural		

Which words mean … ?
1 here, near me
2 there, not near me

d **Sound and spelling** *this*, *that*, *these*, and *those*

1 07.05 Listen to *this*, *that*, *these*, and *those*. Which words … ?
- end in a /s/ sound
- end in a /z/ sound

2 Practice saying the words.

e Now go to Grammar Focus 7A on p. 126.

f You and your partner are in the store below. Talk about the objects in the box with *this*, *that*, *these*, or *those*.

glasses plates speaker plant chairs phone lamp

3 VOCABULARY Prices

a 07.07 Listen to the prices. Check (✓) the phrase you hear.

1 $3.80
 a ☐ three dollar eighty
 b ☐ three dollars eighty cents
 c ☐ three dollars and eighty cents

2 $25
 a ☐ twenty-five dollar
 b ☐ twenty-five dollars
 c ☐ twenty-five of dollars

b 07.08 Practice saying the prices below. Listen and check.

1 $5.99
2 $16.50
3 $4.50
4 $100

c 07.09 Listen. Then complete the conversation.

A Excuse me. [1]________ ________ is that **clock**?
B [2]________ $13.50.
A Hmm. And [3]________ ________ are these **cups**?
B [4]________ $5 each.

d Practice the conversation in 3c with a partner. Change the words in **bold** and the prices.

e How much are these things in your country?

- a cup of coffee in a café
- a phone
- a pizza
- a bottle of water

4 SPEAKING

Communication 7A

Student A go to p. 113.
Student B go to p. 111.

7B IT'S OSCAR'S T-SHIRT

Learn to talk about clothes that people wear

G Possessive *'s*; Review of adverbs

V Clothes; Colors

They make colorful clothes, but do they wear them?

Fashion designers often make very different and interesting clothes for people, but they don't usually wear colorful clothes. They often wear the same clothes and the same colors.

TOM FORD makes beautiful clothes for men and for women, but he often wears a white shirt and a black or dark gray jacket.

1 VOCABULARY Clothes

a Look at the pictures of the models and the fashion designers. Which clothes do you like?

b 07.10 Match the words in the box with a–h in the pictures. Listen and check.

jacket coat shirt skirt pants T-shirt dress blouse

c Which clothes do you often wear together?

d **Sound and spelling** /ʃ/ and /dʒ/

1 07.11 Listen and practice these sounds.
1 /ʃ/ **sh**irt 2 /dʒ/ **j**acket

2 07.12 Look at the words in the box. What sounds do the letters in **bold** have? Listen and add the words to the sound groups below.

German internationa**l** fa**sh**ion lar**g**e langua**g**e **g**ym **s**ugar

Sound 1 /ʃ/	Sound 2 /dʒ/
shirt	jacket

3 Practice saying the words.

e **Communication 7B** Student A go to p. 110. Student B go to p. 114.

2 READING

a Read about the fashion designers. What is the same about them?

b Read the text again. Are the sentences true or false? Correct the false sentences.

1 Fashion designers sometimes wear boring clothes.
2 Tom Ford never wears a black jacket.
3 Carolina Herrera often wears a white skirt.
4 Michael Kors usually wears a jacket.

c Is it a good idea for fashion designers to wear their clothes? Why / Why not?

3 VOCABULARY Colors

a Look at the picture of Tom Ford. Complete the sentence about him with colors in the box.

black ● gray ● white ○

Tom Ford often wears a ________ shirt and a ________ or dark ________ jacket.

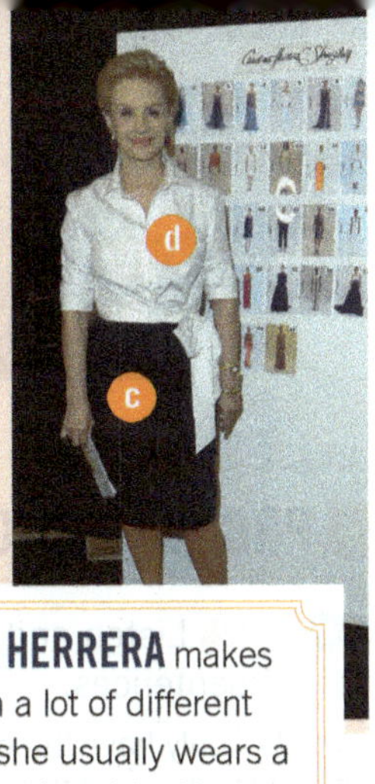

CAROLINA HERRERA makes clothes with a lot of different colors, but she usually wears a black skirt and a white blouse.

MICHAEL KORS designs colorful clothes, but he often wears a black T-shirt, black jeans, and a black jacket.

Language Plus *dark/light*

***dark** blue* ***light** blue*
***dark** green* ***light** green*

b Now go to Vocabulary Focus 7B on p. 148.

c Work with a partner.

Student A: Choose a picture in 1a. Don't tell your partner! Talk about the colors and the clothes.
Student B: Guess the picture your partner talks about.

Then switch roles.

4 LISTENING

a 07.15 Listen to Isabella and Gonzalo López. Check (✓) the clothes you hear.

☐ T-shirt ☐ skirt ☐ shoes
☐ jeans ☐ pants ☐ shirt

b 07.15 Listen again and complete the information.

Who?	What clothes?	Why?
Oscar	______	*doesn't wear / doesn't like*
Sara	______	*doesn't wear / doesn't like*
Gonzalo	______	*doesn't wear / doesn't like*

5 GRAMMAR Possessive *'s*; Review of adverbs

a 07.16 Complete the sentences with a name from 4b. Listen and check.

1 **GONZALO** Is this my old T-shirt?
ISABELLA No, it's ______**'s** T-shirt. (= It's **his** T-shirt.)
2 **GONZALO** Are these your jeans?
ISABELLA No, they're ______**'s** jeans. (= They're **her** jeans.)

b Now go to Grammar Focus 7B on p. 126.

c Look at the picture of Oscar, Sara, Gonzalo, and Isabella. Ask and answer questions about the López family.

Who's Gonzalo?
He's Isabella's husband.

d 07.18 Isabella talks about the people in her office. Put the word in parentheses in the correct place in the sentences. Listen and check.

> Everyone wears different clothes at work. [1]My boss wears a blouse and pants (always). [2]She wears a skirt (never) – she doesn't like them. [3]John wears jeans and a white shirt (usually), [4]but he wears black pants (sometimes). [5]And Lindsay wears a dress (often), [6]but on Fridays she wears jeans (usually).

e Think of people you work or study with. What do they usually wear? Tell a partner.

6 SPEAKING

a Put the words and phrases in the correct order to make questions. Write another question with your own idea.

1 wear / at work (or school) / do you / what ?
2 wear / do you / what color clothes ?
3 your brother's (or sister's, father's, mother's) clothes / do you / wear ?
4 at home / do you / wear shoes ?

b Ask and answer the questions in 6a. Add extra information to your answers.

What do you wear to work?
I usually wear a blue or black dress and dark shoes. I like dark colors.

The López family

7C EVERYDAY ENGLISH
Can I help you?

Learn to ask about and pay for things in a store

P Connecting sounds
W An email request for information

1 LISTENING

a Number the things you can buy from 1 to 4.
1 = I like going shopping for this/these very much.
4 = I really don't like going shopping for this/these.

☐ food ☐ clothes ☐ things for the home ☐ electronics

b Talk with a partner about your ideas in 1a. Do you like shopping for the same things?

c 07.19 Listen to Part 1. Answer the questions.

1 Who do Alexis and Mia go shopping for?
2 What does Mia buy?

d 07.19 Listen to Part 1 again. Complete the information about the things in the store.

Umbrellas	Bags
price: $______ colors: ______ ______	price: $______ colors: ______ ______

2 USEFUL LANGUAGE
Going shopping 1

a 07.20 Who says each expression – the customer (C) or the sales assistant (S)? Listen and check.

1 How much are these umbrellas?
2 I'd like four of these plates, please.
3 They're fifteen dollars each.
4 Sure.
5 Can I look around?
6 Can I help you?
7 Of course.

b 07.21 Put the conversation in the correct order. Listen and check.

☐ It's fifteen dollars.
☐ Of course.
☐ It's ten dollars for the small one.
1 Can I help you?
☐ And how much is the small bowl?
☐ OK, then I'd like the large bowl, please.
☐ Yes, thank you. How much is this large bowl?

c Practice the conversation in 2b with a partner.

d Practice the conversation in 2b again, but ask about glasses. Change the prices.

3 PRONUNCIATION Connecting sounds

a 07.22 Listen and notice the extra sounds in these sentences.

1 We /j/ only have three.
2 I'd like two /w/ of these glasses.

Practice saying the sentences.

b Complete the rules with the sounds in the box.

/w/ /j/

We add a ______ sound between words ending with /i/ and words starting with a vowel.
We add a ______ sound between words ending with /u/ and words starting with a vowel.

c 07.23 Listen to these sentences. Which extra /j/ or /w/ sound can you hear? Listen again and repeat.

1 Would you like two or three?
2 These are for me and you.
3 Would you like three or four?
4 Are they for you or me?

d Practice the sentences in 3c with a partner.

4 LISTENING AND USEFUL LANGUAGE
Going shopping 2

a 07.24 Listen to Part 2. Are the sentences true or false?

1 Mia pays ten dollars.
2 She uses a card to pay.
3 Alexis doesn't buy anything.

b 07.25 Complete the sentences with words in the box. Listen and check.

your   that's   here's   you   no

S OK, ________ eight dollars, please.
C Here ________ go.
S Enter ________ PIN, please.
C OK, ________ problem.
S ________ your receipt.

c 07.26 Complete a conversation between a sales assistant and customer. Use phrases in 4b. Listen and check.

C How much ... ? (*shoes*)
S Thirty dollars.
C Here ...
S Enter ...
C OK ...
S And ... receipt.

d Practice the conversation in 4c with a partner. Change the things you buy and the price.

5 SPEAKING

Communication 7C

Student A go to p. 111.
Student B go to p. 112.

6 WRITING

a Alexis saw an online advertisement.

FOR SALE

Designer women's coats, blouses, jeans, bags – *all in good condition.*
Not expensive!

Email me for more information **stylecarolina@travelmail.com**

Read her email. What information does she want to know?

Dear Carolina,

You have an online ad for things you want to sell. I'd like a bag, a coat, and a blouse. Can I see photos of these things? How much are they? Can I pay by credit card?

Thank you!

Alexis

b Now go to Writing Plus 7C on p. 161 for Commas, exclamation points, and question marks.

c You see these online advertisements.

FOR SALE

Sports T-shirts and balls – lots of different sports – signed by professional players: soccer, basketball, baseball, and more.
Great prices!

Email me for more information **ilovesports@travelmail.com**

FOR SALE

Beautiful things for your home – chairs, lamps, small tables.
All in good condition.

Email me for more information **melissa@travelmail.com**

Write an email to ask about one of the advertisements. Here are some ideas:

You have a / an / some ...
I need ...
How old ... ?
How much ... ?
Can I pay ... ?

d Read a partner's email. What objects does your partner ask about? Do you ask about the same things?

UNIT PROGRESS TEST

CHECK YOUR PROGRESS

YOU CAN NOW DO THE UNIT PROGRESS TEST.

UNIT 7
Review

1 GRAMMAR

a Complete the sentences with the phrases in the box.

these	this	those	that's

1 ______ is my dad's car.

2 I love ______ flowers.

3 ______ an expensive car.

4 ______ flowers in the windows are nice!

b Underline the correct answers to complete the conversation.

ZOE Hi, Lee. Do you know Kate? [1] *This / That / These* are [2] *Kate's / Kates / Kates'* daughters, Amy and Anna.
LEE Hello! Nice to meet you, girls. Who's who?
ZOE This [3] *is / are* Amy.
ANNA And I'm Anna.
LEE I like your bag, Anna.
ANNA Oh, thanks. It's [4] *Amys / Amys' / Amy's*. Amy and I have a swimming lesson today.
ZOE Yes, the [5] *girl's / girls / girls'* lesson starts at nine.
ANNA And then we go to our favorite restaurant!

c Practice the conversation in 1b in groups of three.

2 VOCABULARY

a Complete the names of these common objects.

1 a p______e

2 a g______r

3 a c______r

4 a g______s

5 a l______p

6 a p______t

b Complete the descriptions using the colors and clothes.

white	light blue	light brown	red	green	dark blue

shirt	coat	skirt	jeans	shoes

1 a ______ dress
2 ______ pants and black ______
3 a gray ______ and a ______ jacket
4 a light green ______ and a ______ hat
5 a ______ blouse and a red ______
6 dark blue ______ and a ______ T-shirt

c How many hats/coats/jackets/shoes do you have? What color are they? Tell a partner.

3 SOUND AND SPELLING

a 07.27 Answer the questions. Practice saying the words.

1 Which words have the /k/ sound? Underline them.

suitcase clock place chair cup jacket coat dark

2 Which words have the /p/ sound? Underline them.

pink lamp photograph picture plate plant

3 Which words have the /g/ sound? Underline them.

magazine bag light gray green thing

b 07.28 Complete the chart with the words in the box. Practice saying the words.

shoes	sugar	international	jeans	large
fashion	T-shirt	jacket	Germany	

/ʃ/	/dʒ/
shoes	

REVIEW YOUR PROGRESS

How well did you do in this unit? Write 3, 2, or 1 for each objective.
3 = very well 2 = well 1 = not so well

I CAN ...	
talk about things I want to buy	☐
talk about the clothes that people wear	☐
ask about and pay for things in a store	☐

CAN DO OBJECTIVES

- Talk about past events
- Describe events in the past
- Make and respond to suggestions

UNIT 8

PAST EVENTS

GETTING STARTED

a Look at the picture of a New Year's Eve celebration and talk about the questions.

1 Do you want to go there? Why / Why not?
2 What do you think is happening at this New Year's Eve celebration? Here are some ideas:

☐ music	☐ fireworks
☐ dancing	☐ eating food
☐ shopping	☐ meeting friends

b Talk about the questions.

1 Where were you last New Year's Eve?
2 Who were you with?
3 What things did you do?
4 Did you have fun?

8A I WAS ON TOUR WITH MY BAND

Learn to talk about past events

G Simple past: *be*

V Past time expressions

1 READING

a Look at the events in pictures a–d. Choose one you like and one you don't like. Tell a partner. Say why.

a party

a sports game

c concert

a meeting

b Read about Cara, Antonio, and Ava. Which events in 1a do they talk about?

c Read the texts again. Which cities does each person talk about?

d Talk about Cara, Antonio, and Ava's lives with a partner. Who would you like to meet? Why?

My name's Cara. I'm a photographer. I was in New York three days ago for work, and then I was in Chicago yesterday at a meeting about newspaper photography. Life's busy right now!

"Yesterday I was in Chicago."

The people on our team ...

My name's Antonio Marotto. I'm the doctor for our team. It's a great job – I really like helping our players. I often go away with the team. We were in Miami two weeks ago for a game, and we were in Cleveland last week. It's fun to travel with the team.

Ava on the road ...

Hi everyone, it's Ava. Last week I was on tour with my band in the U.S. – three cities in five days. We were in Seattle on Wednesday, and then we were in Portland on Thursday. But Saturday was the best night. We were in San Francisco, and about 1,000 people were at our concert.

2 GRAMMAR Simple past: *be* affirmative

a Complete the chart. Find examples of the simple past of *be* in the texts about Cara, Antonio, and Ava.

+	
I [1] ______ you were he/she/it [2] ______	we [3] ______ you were they were

b 08.01 **Pronunciation** Listen to sentences 1–4. Are *was* and *were* stressed? Practice saying the sentences.

1 We were in Seattle.
2 I was in Los Angeles.
3 We were in Miami.
4 I was in New York.

c Now go to Grammar Focus 8A Part 1 on p. 128.

d Write sentences about where you were:

- this morning
- last night
- yesterday afternoon

e Compare your sentences in 2d with a partner. Were you in the same places?

Juan and I were at the supermarket yesterday.

3 VOCABULARY Past time expressions

a Today is Friday of week 3. Put the number of sentences 1–4 in the correct place on the timeline.

week 1	week 2	week 3
		Monday Tuesday Wednesday Thursday (Friday)

1 We were in Seattle on <u>Wednesday</u>.
2 We were in Miami two <u>weeks</u> ago.
3 … we were in Cleveland last <u>week</u>.
4 I was in Chicago <u>yesterday</u>.

b Look at the <u>underlined</u> words in 3a. Replace them with words in the box.

months   this morning   Saturday   year

c Now go to Vocabulary Focus 8A on p. 149.

d Work in pairs.
Student A: Say a past time expression.
Student B: Say where a person you know was.
Then switch roles.

last weekend

My parents were in London last weekend.

two years ago

My friend Marco was in Ecuador two years ago.

4 LISTENING AND GRAMMAR Simple past: *be* negative and questions

a 08.06 Review the texts about Cara, Antonio, and Ava again. Then listen to them talking to friends. Write the correct name for each conversation.

Conversation 1 ______
Conversation 2 ______
Conversation 3 ______

b 08.06 Match events 1–3 with adjectives a–c. Listen again and check.

1 the meeting   a exciting
2 the game   b interesting
3 the concert   c fun

c 08.07 Listen to Conversation 1 again. Complete the conversation with the words in the box.

was (x2)   were (x2)   wasn't

WILL ______ you at work yesterday?
CARA Yes, I ______, but I ______ here in the office.
WILL Where ______ you?
CARA I was at a meeting in Chicago.
WILL Oh, ______ it interesting?
CARA Yes, it was really interesting.

d Now go to Grammar Focus 8A Part 2 on p. 128.

e 08.11 Complete the conversation with *was, were, wasn't,* or *weren't*. Listen and check.

A You ______ at work yesterday.
B No, I ______ off yesterday.
A Nice. ______ you at home all day?
B No, I ______. I ______ in town in the morning, and then I ______ at a party last night.
A ______ the party good?
B Yes, it ______ a lot of fun.

f Practice the conversation in 4e with a partner. Change some of the information.

I was at a baseball game in the morning and then at the movies last night.

Was the movie good?

5 SPEAKING

a **Communication 8A** Student A go to p. 113. Student B go to p. 111. Student C go to p. 115.

8B HE SAW A BEAR

Learn to describe events in the past

- **G** Simple past: affirmative
- **V** Free time activities

1 READING

a Look at pictures 1–3 below. Match the pictures to the animal names. Where do they usually live? What do you know about them?

_____ deer _____ bear _____ hippo

b Read the stories below. Write the story titles next to the sentences.

1 Hippos were on a rugby field. __________
2 Three deer were in a woman's apartment. __________
3 A bear was in a man's backyard. __________

c Read the stories again. Complete the information.

	Where?	When?	Animal activity?
Andrew from Utah	at home		
Ben from South Africa		evening	
A woman from Indiana			jump

d Talk about the questions.

1 Which story do you like?
2 Which animals sometimes come into houses in your country?

cat

dog

bird

snake

3 What do you do if a wild animal comes to your house?

WILD STORIES!

1

CURIOUS CREATURE

Andrew Singer from Utah was at home in his house on a farm. One evening he was in the kitchen, and he heard something strange in the backyard, so he looked out the window. He saw a bear in the backyard. The bear walked around the backyard and looked in the windows of the house. It tried to open the kitchen door, and the man was really scared. It wasn't possible for the bear to get in, so it went away. The man thinks the bear was hungry, but it's not a good idea to give bears food.

2

SURPRISE VISITORS

A woman from Indiana had an apartment with a yard. In the evening, she went into her living room and watched TV. She heard something in her bedroom, so she went to look. She saw three deer near her bed. They came into the living room and jumped on her sofa, then they went into the bathroom. The woman called 911, and the police came to catch the deer. She had an exciting night with her three new friends!

3

READY TO PLAY

Ben Kruger from South Africa loves playing rugby. He has a business in Limpopo, a city in the north of South Africa. One night after work, he went to a rugby field nearby. It was dark, and he saw something on the field. It was large, but it wasn't a person – it was a hippopotamus (hippo)! Then he saw another hippo and then another – there were a lot of them. The hippos ate some grass and then went away. Ben thinks the hippos were from a river near the rugby field.

2 GRAMMAR Simple past: affirmative

a 08.12 Read the stories again and find the simple past forms of the verbs in the chart. Listen and check.

A		B	
Verb	**Past form**	**Verb**	**Past form**
look	*looked*	have	*had*
watch		hear	
call		eat	
jump		see	
walk		go	
try		come	

b Answer the questions about the chart in 2a.

1 What do we add to the verbs in A to make the past form?
2 Do the verbs in B all change in the same way or in different ways?

c **Sound and spelling** /t/ and /d/

1 08.13 Listen and practice these sounds.
1 /t/ talk**ed** 2 /d/ live**d**

2 08.14 Listen to the past forms in the box. Which *-ed* endings sound … ?
• more like /t/ • more like /d/

looked watched called tried
walked played finished

3 Practice saying the words.

d Cover the chart in 2a. Test a partner.
Student A: Say a verb.
Student B: Say the past form.
Then switch roles.

e Now go to Grammar Focus 8B on p. 128.

f Complete the sentences so they are true for you.

1 Yesterday I called ____________. (a person)
2 Last month I saw ____________. (a TV show)
3 Last weekend I went to ____________. (a place)
4 Last night I ate ____________. (food)

Tell your partner about your sentences.

3 LISTENING AND VOCABULARY Free time activities

a 08.17 Listen to three conversations about the three stories. In each conversation, some information is incorrect. What is the wrong information?

1 ____________
2 ____________
3 ____________

b 08.18 Listen to the sentences from the conversations. Use the correct verb in the box.

read (x2) talked went had watched heard

1 I just ________ to a café.
2 I ________ a large coffee.
3 And I ________ the newspaper.
4 I ________ this funny story.
5 I ________ this story on a podcast.
6 I ________ to my friend Katie last night.
7 She ________ the video online.

c Match verbs 1 to 6 with a word or phrase in the box to make more simple past phrases.

a book to my parents home dinner a movie
for a walk breakfast a song on the radio to my friend

1 went ______, ______
2 had ______, ______
3 read ______
4 heard ______
5 talked ______, ______
6 watched ______

d 08.19 Listen to Emily talk about the things she did yesterday. Put pictures a–e in the correct order.

e 08.19 Complete what Emily says with phrases from 3c. Then listen again and check.

Yesterday I [1]__________ at about 9:00, and then I went to a café and had coffee with my friend Karen. After that, I went to work and was there all day. I [2]__________ with my brother, and then I [3]__________ and called my parents. I [4]__________ Rosie in Brazil on Skype. After, I [5]__________ online, and then I went to bed and [6]__________ before going to sleep.

f Now go to Vocabulary Focus 8B on p. 150.

g Complete the sentences about free time activities.

1 When I was a child, I ______.
2 After work / school, I often ______.
3 On weekends, I like to ______.

h Tell other students your sentences in 3g. What free time activities were/are popular … ?

a when everyone was a child
b after work / school
c on weekends

4 SPEAKING

a **Communication 8B** Student A go to p. 113. Student B go to p. 111.

8C EVERYDAY ENGLISH

Let's go somewhere this weekend

Learn to make and respond to suggestions

P Sentence stress and intonation

W Thank you note

1 LISTENING

a Ask and answer the questions.

1 On the first day at work / school after the weekend, how do you feel?
2 What do you usually talk to your friends about on that day?

b 08.22 Listen to Part 1. Logan and Daniel are at work on Monday morning. Check (✓) the things they talk about:

a ☐ the weekend
b ☐ Boston (the city where they live)
c ☐ work
d ☐ family
e ☐ baseball

c 08.22 Listen to Part 1 again. Are the sentences true or false?

1 Daniel was busy with friends all weekend.
2 Logan likes the city, but he doesn't like the weather.
3 Logan sees his family often.

d What do you like about the town or city where you live? What don't you like?

e 08.23 Listen to Part 2. Who went to a party? Who watched TV?

f 08.23 Listen to Part 2 again and answer the questions.

1 What's difficult for Logan? Is it hard for Daniel, too?
2 What's Daniel's idea for next weekend?
3 Does Logan feel happy or sad at the end of the conversation? Why?

g Talk about the questions.

1 Is it difficult to meet new people in your town / city? Why / Why not?
2 What are good ways to meet new people?

Boston, Massachusetts

2 USEFUL LANGUAGE Making and responding to suggestions

a 08.24 Listen to the conversations. Underline the word you hear. Are both options possible?

1 **DANIEL** *Let's / We could* go to Newport.
LOGAN That sounds *nice / good.*
2 **DANIEL** So, *do you want to / let's* go there on Saturday?
LOGAN Yeah, that's a *nice / great* idea.

b 08.25 Complete the conversation with the words in the box. Listen and check.

A Let's ______ for dinner on Saturday.
B Saturday? I'm ______, I can't. I'm out of town on Saturday.
A Do you ______ to go on Sunday?
B Yes, that's a great ______.

want idea go sorry

c Practice the conversation in 2b with a partner.

d Complete the conversation with words or expressions in 2a and 2b. There is sometimes more than one answer.

A ______ go to the movies tonight.
B ______, I'm busy. I have a work dinner.
A ______ go tomorrow night.
B OK, ______.

e Practice the conversation in 2d with a partner. Take turns being A and B.

3 PRONUNCIATION Sentence stress and intonation

a 08.26 Listen to the expressions. Notice the main stress.

1 Yes, that's a great idea. 2 Yes, that's a nice idea.

b 08.26 Listen to the expressions in 3a again. Does the intonation rise ↗ or fall ↘ after the main stress?

c Work with a partner.

Student A: Say sentences 1 and 2.
Student B: Answer with phrases in 3a.
1 Let's have some coffee.
2 Do you want to go for a walk?

Then switch roles.

4 SPEAKING

a Work in pairs. Read the ideas below and think about what you want to say.

A	B
Suggest going to a restaurant on Friday.	You're busy on Friday. You have a work dinner.
Suggest Saturday.	Say yes. Suggest an Italian restaurant.
You went to an Italian restaurant last weekend. Suggest a Mexican restaurant.	Say yes. Suggest a time.
Agree with Student B. Say goodbye.	Thank Student A and say goodbye.

b Have a phone conversation with your partner. Then switch roles.

Do you want to go to a restaurant on Friday?

I'm sorry, I'm busy that night. I have a work dinner.

5 WRITING

a Read Logan's text to Daniel. Why did Logan write it?

b Now go to Writing Plus 8C on p. 161 for Writing short emails, notes, and texts.

c Write a note to a friend to thank them for something. Here are some ideas:

I want to say thank you for …
It was …
I hope …

d Read another student's note. What do they say thank you for?

UNIT PROGRESS TEST

CHECK YOUR PROGRESS

YOU CAN NOW DO THE UNIT PROGRESS TEST.

UNIT 8
Review

1 GRAMMAR

a Write simple past sentences and questions with *be* and the words and phrases.

> (?) where / you yesterday
Where were you yesterday?
1 (+) I / in a meeting.
2 (?) / you OK
3 (–) James / at work this morning.
4 (?) where / he
5 (+) Yasmin and Kylie / in New York two weeks ago.
6 (–) we / in Paris six years ago

b Complete the text with the simple past form of the verb in parentheses.

Last week my family and I [1]__________ (be) in Miami. We [2]__________ (arrive) on Wednesday morning. First, we [3]__________ (visit) my dad's family. My dad and his brothers [4]__________ (talk) for a long time. Then we [5]__________ (go) to a big museum in downtown Miami. We [6]__________ (see) a lot of interesting things there. In the evening, we [7]__________ (watch) a movie. We [8]__________ (stay) at the Dylan Hotel. The rooms [9]__________ (not / be) very big, but I [10]__________ (like) the bathroom and the food [11]__________ (be) great! Every morning I [12]__________ (have) toast, eggs, fruit, and coffee for breakfast.

2 VOCABULARY

a Check (✓) the correct answer.

Today is WEDNESDAY, OCTOBER 21. It's 7:30 p.m.

1 Wednesday, October 7
a ☐ two weeks ago
b ☐ yesterday
2 2:30 p.m. on Wednesday, October 21
a ☐ last night
b ☐ this afternoon
3 August 21
a ☐ two months ago
b ☐ last month
4 Tuesday, October 20
a ☐ yesterday
b ☐ a few days ago
5 Saturday, October 17
a ☐ this morning
b ☐ last Saturday
6 Sunday, October 18
a ☐ six months ago
b ☐ on Sunday

b Ask and answer questions with *Where were you … ?* and a past time expression.

c Complete the chart with the words and phrases in the box.

a video game a soccer game (x2)
a magazine a pizza a podcast a shower

have	a drink, coffee, [1]__________
listen to	music, [2]__________
watch	[3]__________, a movie
read	a book, [4]__________, the newspaper
play	the guitar, [5]__________, soccer
go to	the movies, a party, [6]__________, a café
take	[7]__________

d Correct the sentences.

1 I was in Atlanta before two weeks ago.
2 We were in Quito last the weekend.
3 I had coffee with Lily at Friday.
4 We went a party yesterday.
5 I listened music last night.
6 We played the baseball this morning.

3 SOUND AND SPELLING

a 08.27 Look at the words in the box. Is the final sound /t/ or /d/? Complete the chart. Practice saying the words.

~~called~~ talked lived watched
listened played finished

/t/	/d/
	called

b 08.28 Listen to the sentences. Underline the word with the main stress.

1 That's a great idea.
2 It's a beautiful place.
3 It was good.
4 How was your weekend?

c Complete the conversation with the phrases from 3b. Then practice with a partner.

A Good morning! [1]
B [2]__________ I stayed at home and watched movies. What about you?
A On Saturday, I went to a new park in my city. [3]__________.
B [4]__________ Saturday was a beautiful day.
A Yes, it was.

REVIEW YOUR PROGRESS

How well did you do in this unit? Write 3, 2, or 1 for each objective.
3 = very well 2 = well 1 = not so well

I CAN ...	
talk about past events	☐
describe events in the past	☐
make and respond to suggestions	☐

CAN DO OBJECTIVES

- Talk about travel and vacation experiences
- Talk about past vacations
- Make and respond to requests

UNIT 9

VACATIONS

GETTING STARTED

a Look at the picture and answer the questions.

1 What country do you think this is?
2 What transportation can you see?
3 What time of year is it?
4 What is the weather like in this place?

b Talk about the questions.

1 Where did you go on your last vacation?
2 What weather do you like while on vacation? Why?

c Ask your partner one question about their last vacation.

9A I DIDN'T STAY IN A HOTEL

Learn to talk about travel and vacation experiences

G Simple past: negative

V Transportation

BACKYARD CAMPING

Home | Find A Backyard | Reviews | Contact Us

How Does It Work?

Do you want a cheap vacation in a beautiful place? Why not camp in someone's backyard? It's cheap, and you can make new friends. We have more than 1,000 backyards in 70 countries, and you can camp in all of them!

Old house with a big backyard on a lake. 20 minutes from the Salt Lake City airport.

COST $15 a night

HOW TO GET THERE
Go to Stansbury Park by bus or tram. Then take a taxi or drive a car to the house (5 minutes).

ROBERT'S PLACE, STANSBURY PARK, UTAH, U.S.

42 big tents with beds and showers inside. 40 minutes from the city of Marrakesh.

COST $30 a night

HOW TO GET THERE
Fly to Marrakesh and then take a taxi or drive a car.

YOUSSEF'S PLACE, MARRAKESH, MOROCCO

1 READING

a Where do you usually stay on vacation? Here are some ideas:

- at a hotel
- at a hostel
- at a campsite
- with friends or family

b Read *How Does It Work?* on the *Backyard Camping* website. What do you think of the idea?

It's a great idea!

Hmm, interesting.

No, thanks!

c Read about three backyards on the *Backyard Camping* website. Which answers (a–d) are incorrect? Correct the wrong answers.

1 Robert's place:
  a old house
  b big backyard
  c in Salt Lake City
  d near the bus station

2 Youssef's place:
  a small tents
  b showers
  c not in Marrakesh
  d not very cheap

3 Guadalupe's place:
  a big backyard
  b pool
  c near some restaurants
  d expensive

2 VOCABULARY Transportation

a 09.01 Find words on the *Backyard Camping* website to match pictures 1–7. Listen and check.

b Find words on the *Backyard Camping* website to complete the charts.

go ______	bus plane tram

______	a bus a taxi

c Find verbs in the texts that mean:
a go by car
b go by plane

d Now go to Vocabulary Focus 9A on p. 151.

e How do you ... ?
1 go to work or school
2 go to a big town or city nearby
3 go home late at night
4 go to a party
5 go on vacation

I usually take a bus to work.

House with a big backyard and swimming pool. Free bikes. Near restaurants, a river, and a zoo.

COST: $4 a night

HOW TO GET THERE: Go to Villavicencio by plane or bus. Then take a taxi or another bus to our house.

GUADALUPE'S PLACE, CUMARAL, COLOMBIA

Language Plus *go*

go *to the movies*

go *to work* NOT ~~*to the work*~~

go *home* NOT ~~*to home*~~

go *on vacation*

f **Sound and spelling** the letter *a*

1 09.04 The letter *a* can have different sounds. Listen and practice the words.
1 /æ/ taxi 2 /ɑ/ car 3 /eɪ/ plane

2 09.05 Listen to these words. Are the letters in **bold** Sound 1, 2, or 3?

w**a**nt c**a**mp tr**a**in f**a**ther

3 09.06 Listen to these words. Which one in each group has a different *a* sound?

1 tr**a**m	w**a**nt	m**a**n
2 h**a**ve	l**a**ke	v**a**cation
3 p**a**rty	b**a**g	b**a**ckyard
4 pl**a**nt	gl**a**ss	w**a**nt

4 Practice saying the words.

3 GRAMMAR AND LISTENING
Simple past: negative

a Read the post from Julian's travel blog. Which place from the *Backyard Camping* website does he write about?

Julian

WEEK 3

Through the Country by Bus

We didn't go to big cities. We went by bus, and we stayed in small places in the country. In one place, we stayed with a family. We didn't stay in their house – we camped in their backyard. We bought food in the town, and we cooked meals in the house. And we went swimming every morning in their pool. It was very cheap, and the family was very friendly. We stayed for four days!

15 7

b Read the blog post again. Check (✓) the correct sentences.

1 a ☐ They went to small places.
b ☐ They didn't go to small places.
2 a ☐ They had a car.
b ☐ They didn't have a car.
3 a ☐ They stayed in the house.
b ☐ They didn't stay in the house.
4 a ☐ They used the kitchen.
b ☐ They didn't use the kitchen.

c Look at the b sentences in 3b. Complete the rule.

Simple past negative (–):
I/you/he/she/it/we/they + ________ + verb

d Now go to Grammar Focus 9A on p. 130.

e 09.08 **Pronunciation** Listen to the sentences. Is *didn't* stressed or unstressed?

1 We didn't stay in their house.
2 We didn't have a car.

f 09.09 Listen to Julian. He says more things about his trip. What does he say about … ?

- emails
- money
- bikes
- photos

g What do you like about Julian's vacation? What don't you like?

h Think about your last vacation. Which sentences are true? If they aren't true, make them negative. Then write a true affirmative sentence.

1 I stayed in a hotel.
2 I visited museums.
3 I bought a lot of clothes.
4 I had my computer with me.
5 I went to bed early.
6 I cooked my own food.
7 I watched TV.
8 I read a lot of books.

1 *I didn't stay in a hotel. I stayed in a hostel.*

i Tell a partner your sentences in 3h.

I didn't visit museums. I went to the zoo.

4 SPEAKING

Communication 9A Student A go to p. 114. Student B go to p. 110.

9B HOW DID YOU GET THERE?

Learn to talk about past vacations

G Simple past: questions

V The seasons; The weather

1 VOCABULARY The seasons

a 09.10 Match the words in the box with pictures a–d. Listen and check.

winter	summer	spring	autumn / fall

a

b

c

d

b Ask and answer the questions.

1 Do you have four seasons in your country?
2 Which seasons do you like? Which seasons don't you like?

2 READING

a Read about the Ortega family's vacation. What was different about this New Year's Eve and New Year's Day for them?

b Complete Michael's notes with the words in the box.

party	shopping	watched	cold

< Notes Done

Thursday: [1] ____________ with family in Union Square

New Year's Eve: [2] ____________ in Times Square – great fireworks!

Friday: [3] ____________ and snowy weather; everyone stayed inside and [4] ____________ a movie.

The Ortega family from Puerto Rico went to New York City for New Year's Eve. Read Michael Ortega's blog post.

MY BLOG

MICHAEL ORTEGA

New Year's Fun in the BIG APPLE

Times Square ball drop

Thursday, December 31

We went shopping in Union Square – it has a lot of big stores, restaurants, and cafés. The weather is cold and windy in December, but we enjoyed it! We went to a big New Year's Eve party in Times Square in the evening and watched the ball drop. My sister and I loved the fireworks!

Friday, January 1

It's winter here, and it's very different to have our New Year's in the cold. I like the hot, sunny weather in Puerto Rico on New Year's Day, but in New York it was very cold and snowy. It didn't feel like New Year's Day. Everyone stayed inside and watched a movie!

3 VOCABULARY The weather

a 09.11 What does Michael say about the weather in New York City and Puerto Rico? Complete the sentences with *hot* or *cold*. Listen and check.

1 The weather is _______ and windy in December.

2 I like the _______, sunny weather in Puerto Rico on New Year's Day.

> **Language Plus** *like*
>
> *I **like** sunny weather.* = I think sunny weather is good.
> *What's the weather **like**?* = How's the weather?

b Now go to Vocabulary Focus 9B on p. 152.

c **Sound and spelling** the letter *o*

1 09.14 The letter *o* can have different sounds. Listen and repeat the words.
1 /oʊ/ sn**o**w 2 /aʊ/ cl**o**udy 3 /ɑ/ h**o**t

2 09.15 Listen to these words. Are the letters in **bold** Sound 1, 2, or 3?

sh**o**pping t**o**wn c**o**ld

3 09.16 Listen to these words. Which one in each group has a different *o* sound? Listen again and repeat.

1	g**o**t	j**o**b	g**o**
2	kn**o**w	n**o**t	sl**o**w
3	ph**o**ne	n**o**w	d**o**wn

d **Communication 9B** Student A go to p. 111. Student B go to p. 113.

4 LISTENING AND GRAMMAR Simple past: questions

a 09.17 Listen to Eric and Angie talk about summer vacations. Check (✓) the correct sentence.

1 ☐ They're on vacation now.
2 ☐ They talk about past and future vacations.
3 ☐ They only talk about past vacations.

b 09.17 Listen again. Match 1–3 with a–c.

1 Eric last year a San Andrés Island
2 Angie last year b Uruguay
3 Angie two years ago c São Paulo

c 09.18 Listen to the end of the conversation. Choose one word from the box to complete the two questions.

do did

Eric How _______ you get there?
Angie By bus. And, you know, the weather was really warm.
Eric _______ you enjoy it there?
Angie Yes, I did. I had a great time, and I didn't want to leave!

d Now go to Grammar Focus 9B on p. 130.

e 09.21 Complete the two conversations about last weekend. Listen and check your answers.

Conversation 1
A go / movies last weekend?
B Yes, I did.
A What / see?
B The new James Bond movie.

Conversation 2
C go / restaurant last night?
D Yes, I did.
C Where / go?
D A new Thai restaurant.

f Tell a partner about last weekend. Use the conversations in 4e and your own ideas.

Did you see your friends last weekend?
Yes, I did.
Who did you see?
I saw Daniele.

g Work in new pairs. Tell your new partner about your first partner.

Jacob saw his friend Daniele last weekend.

5 SPEAKING

a Think about a past vacation. Write notes about the:

- place
- weather
- food
- things you did

b Write questions to ask about your partner's vacation.

1 When … the vacation? *When was the vacation?*
2 Where … go?
3 What … the weather like?
4 What … eat?
5 What … do?
6 (your idea for a question)

c Ask and answer the questions in 5b about your vacation.

When was the vacation?
It was last spring.
Where did you go?
We went to Lombok, in Indonesia.
What was the weather like?
It was hot and sunny.

9C EVERYDAY ENGLISH

Can you do something for me?

Learn to make and respond to requests

P Syllables

W An online post

1 LISTENING

a Talk about a place near your town or city with a partner. Ask and answer the questions.

1 Where's a nice place to visit for a day? Why?
2 What can you see and do there?
3 Do you go there often?

b 09.22 Look at pictures a and b and talk about the questions. Listen to Part 1 and check your answers.

1 Do you think Isabel and Sara like Mexico?
2 What is the first thing Sara buys at the market?

c 09.22 Listen to Part 1 again. Are the sentences true or false?

1 Isabel doesn't like the food.
2 Sara buys a hat, blankets, and bowls.
3 Sara's bag is heavy and difficult to carry.

d What do you buy when you visit another place?

2 PRONUNCIATION Syllables and spelling

a 09.23 Listen to the word in **bold** in the sentence. Do you hear all the letters?

It's very **different** from Baltimore.

09.23 Listen again and repeat the word in **bold**.

b 09.24 Listen to these words. Underline the letters you don't hear.

restaurant interesting favorite business
every family vegetable camera

c Practice saying the words in 2b.

3 LISTENING

a 09.25 Sara and Isabel are now at the hotel. Listen to Part 2 and check your answers.

1 What does Sara do on her phone?
2 Why can't they take the bus or the subway?

b 09.25 Listen to Part 2 again. Underline the correct answer.

1 Isabel wants to buy something at the *hotel / airport*.
2 Isabel puts Sara's new *blankets / bowls* in her suitcase.
3 Sara *asks / doesn't ask* Isabel for help with her bags.

c Who do you usually ask for help – a friend or someone in your family? Why?

a

b

c

4 USEFUL LANGUAGE Making and responding to requests

a 09.26 Listen to the questions. Underline the word you hear. Then answer the question below.

1 *Can / Could* you take it for a minute?
2 *Can / Could* you do something for me?
3 *Can / Could* you put these blankets in your suitcase?
4 *Can / Could* you help me with these bags, please?

Is it OK to use *can* and *could* in all the sentences?

b 09.27 Put the possible replies to the questions in 4a into the chart. Listen and check your answers.

Of course. No, I can't.
I'm sorry, I can't. Sure, no problem.

Yes	No

c 09.28 Complete mini-conversations 1 and 2 with the phrases in the box. Listen and check.

Oh, that's OK. I can do it.
Thanks, that's really nice of you.

1 **A** Could you help me with dinner?
B Sure, no problem.
A _______.

2 **C** Can you drive my sister to the train station?
D I'm sorry, I can't. I have a lot of work to finish.
C _______.

d Work in pairs. Take turns making requests and replying. Use the ideas below and *can/could.*

1 help me with my homework
2 give me your book
3 meet me after class
4 call me tonight

Could you meet me after class?

I'm sorry, I can't. I'm busy.

5 SPEAKING

a Work in pairs. You and your partner are on the phone. Look at the ideas below and think about what you want to say.

A / **B**

A: Say hello and who you are.
B: Say hello and ask how Student A is.
A: Answer. Ask for help with something.
B: Say yes.
A: Ask Student B to come shopping with you today.
B: Say no – you're busy today.
A: Ask about tomorrow.
B: Say yes.
A: Say thanks and goodbye.
B: Say goodbye.

b Have a phone conversation with your partner. Then switch roles.

6 WRITING

a Read about Sara's trip. What information about her trip to Mexico is new?

Last week I went to Mexico with Isabel. The last day was my favorite day. First, we went for a walk to the old part of the city. It was beautiful. Next, we had lunch at a small restaurant. The food was great! Then, we went shopping at a market, and I saw some beautiful things. I bought blankets, bowls, and a big hat. Isabel helped me with my bags because they were very heavy! Mexico is a great country – it's very different from Baltimore.

12 3

b Now go to Writing Plus 9C on p. 162 for Making the order clear.

c Write an online post about a trip to another place. Here are some ideas:

Last weekend, / month, / summer, I went to … with …
First, we … It was … Next, we … Then, we …
… is a nice / beautiful / great city / town / place.

d Read another student's online post. Do you like the activities he/she did?

UNIT PROGRESS TEST

CHECK YOUR PROGRESS

YOU CAN NOW DO THE UNIT PROGRESS TEST.

UNIT 9
Review

1 GRAMMAR

a Underline the correct answer.

1 We didn't *stay / stayed* in a hotel last year.
2 I didn't *take / took* any photos this morning.
3 She *doesn't / didn't* buy a book yesterday.
4 They didn't *have / had* fish for dinner last night.
5 We *don't watched / didn't watch* a movie last week.
6 He *didn't took / didn't take* a taxi to the airport.

b Look at the answers and complete the questions.

> "Did it rain yesterday?" "Yes, it did. It rained in the morning."
1 "__________ basketball last week?" "No, I didn't – but I played tennis!"
2 "What time __________ yesterday?" "I got up at six o'clock."
3 "__________ any photos on New Year's Eve?" "Yes, I did. I took some photos at the party."
4 "Where __________ yesterday?" "I went to the park."
5 "__________ your phone yesterday?" "Yes, of course! I use my phone every day!"
6 "What __________ for breakfast today?" "I had cereal and coffee."

c Work in pairs. Ask and answer the questions in 1b.

d Correct the simple past sentences.

> Where they did stay? *Where did they stay?*
1 Do you arrived last night?
2 Yes, I do arrived.
3 No, I not.
4 What did you bought?
5 I didn't watched TV.
6 What you cooked?
7 We don't visit Pedro yesterday.
8 Saw you the backyard?

2 VOCABULARY

a Write the words.

1 ritan __________
2 atix __________
3 bysauw __________
4 mart __________
5 elnap __________
6 pish __________

b Underline the correct answers.

A Was it [1]*cold / wet / warm*?
B Yes! It was –10°C! There was a lot of [2]*snow / snowy*.
A Wow! It never [3]*snows / snowy* in my country.
C Do I need an umbrella?
D I don't know. It's [4]*rainy / rain* – but it's very [5]*wind / windy*, too!
E Was it [6]*wet / hot*?
F Yes, very! It was about 35°C! But it was [7]*cloud / cloudy* all the time. We didn't see the sun.

3 SOUND AND SPELLING

a 09.29 Which of the letters in **bold** in each group has a different sound? Underline the word. Practice saying the words.

1 tr**ai**n c**a**r pl**a**ne r**ai**n
2 c**a**mp w**a**nt h**o**t n**o**t
3 g**o** b**oa**t sn**ow** t**ow**n
4 m**a**n c**a**mp t**a**ke tr**a**m
5 cl**ou**d h**o**me c**o**ld n**o**
6 cl**ou**d n**ow** dr**o**ve d**ow**n

b 09.30 Complete the chart with words in the box.

~~yesterday~~ beautiful ~~different~~ expensive interesting camera every difficult restaurant business favorite museum

We always say all the letters	We don't always say all the letters
yesterday	different

REVIEW YOUR PROGRESS

How well did you do in this unit? Write 3, 2, or 1 for each objective.
3 = very well 2 = well 1 = not so well

I CAN ...	
talk about travel and vacation experiences	☐
talk about past vacations	☐
make and respond to requests	☐

CAN DO OBJECTIVES

- Talk about your home
- Ask where people are and what they're doing
- Ask for travel information

UNIT 10

HERE AND NOW

GETTING STARTED

a Look at the picture and answer the questions.

1 What is the boy doing?
2 Who is the woman? Where is she?
3 What do you think they're saying?
4 How often do you think they do this?
5 How do they feel? Why?

b Talk about the questions.

1 Do you speak to family and friends online? How often? Who do you speak to?
2 What programs or apps do you use to talk to people online?
3 What are the good things and bad things about using the Internet to speak to people?

10A WE'RE WATCHING THE GAME

Learn to talk about your home

- **G** Present continuous: affirmative
- **V** The home

1 VOCABULARY The home

a 10.01 Match the words in the box with pictures a–f. Listen and check.

bedroom yard living room
dining room kitchen bathroom

b Now go to Vocabulary Focus 10A on p. 153.

c Sound and spelling /tʃ/ and /θ/

1. 10.03 Listen and practice these sounds.
   1 /tʃ/ kit**ch**en 2 /θ/ ba**th**room
2. 10.04 What sound do you hear in the words in the box, Sound 1 or Sound 2? Listen and add the words to the sound groups below.

   cheese month birthday thanks change
   both March question three watch

Sound 1 /tʃ/	Sound 2 /θ/
kitchen	bathroom

3. Which letters usually spell /tʃ/ and which spell /θ/?
4. Practice saying the words.

d Ask and answer the questions with a partner.

1. How many bedrooms are there in your home?
2. Where do you eat your dinner?
3. Is there a TV in your home? Where?
4. Do you have a yard? If yes, is it big or small?
5. Which room is your favorite?

2 LISTENING AND SPEAKING

a 10.05 Listen to Grace talk about her apartment. Put pictures a–c on page 81 in the order Grace talks about them.

b 10.05 Listen again. Are the sentences true or false?

1. Grace's apartment isn't big.
2. The light in her apartment is good.
3. There isn't a TV in the living room.
4. There's a dining room in her apartment.
5. She uses her computer in her living room.

c Do you like Grace's apartment? Why / Why not?

Language Plus *in / on*

in + room	***on*** + floor, wall
*There's a desk **in** my bedroom.*	*The books are **on** the floor.*
*Put the cake **in** the kitchen.*	*There are pictures **on** the wall.*

d Think about your home and the rooms it has. Tell a partner about your home.

> In my home, there are four bedrooms and a big bathroom.

e Choose a room in your home and write the names of some objects in that room. Then tell your partner about them.

> In my bedroom, there's a bed, a chair, and a small desk.

3 READING

a Read the texts. Are they for people who are near or far away?

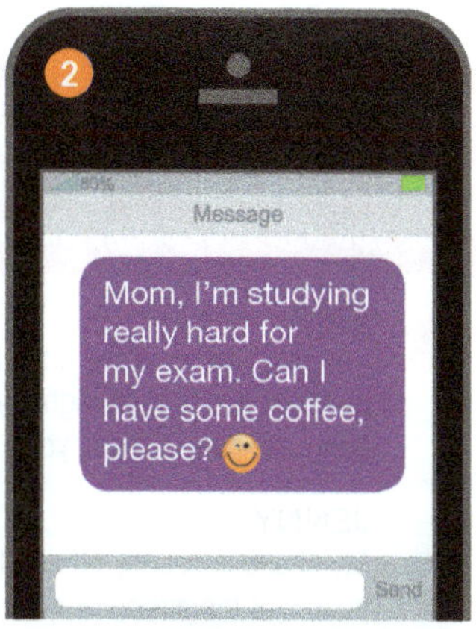

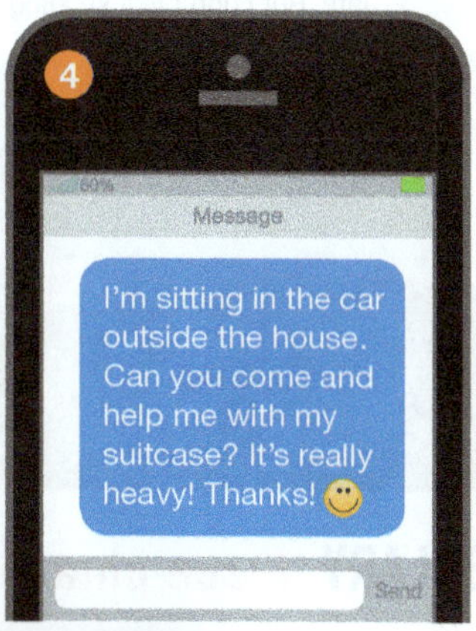

b Read the texts again. Where are the writers?

c Do you sometimes send a text to someone when you're in the same place? Why / Why not?

4 GRAMMAR

Present continuous: affirmative

a Look at the sentence from text 1. Does it mean *now* or *usually*?

We're watching the game.

b Complete the rule with *-ing* and *be*.

> Present continuous affirmative (+):
> *I/you/he/she/it/we/they* + ______ + verb + ______

c 10.06 **Pronunciation** Listen to the sentence in 4a. Underline the stressed words.

d Underline four more examples of the present continuous in texts 2–5 in 3a.

e >>> Now go to Grammar Focus 10A on p. 130.

f It's 2 p.m. on Sunday. What are you doing? Write a text to a friend.

Hi!
I'm having lunch at a new restaurant downtown with my sister. It's really good! We're eating a lot of food.

g Read your text to the class. Listen to the other students. Is anyone doing the same thing?

5 SPEAKING

>>> **Communication 10A** Student A go to p. 115. Student B go to p. 112.

10B ARE YOU WORKING?

Learn to ask where people are and what they're doing

G Present continuous: negative and questions

V Place phrases with prepositions

How much do you use your phone?

Some people always have their phone on, and they use it all the time — in a café, in the car, even in bed! Is this a good idea? Tell us what you think! And do you use your phone all the time?

RAOUL
My phone's always on, day and night, and I use it all the time – I talk on it, play games on it, send messages. When I wake up, I sit in bed, check my messages, and read the news on my phone. It's a great way to start the day!

YASMIN
I never talk on the phone when I'm with people in a restaurant. I have it on "silent" and put it in my bag – I don't want to talk while I'm eating. But I often take photos of the food with it. It's always by my bed at night, so I can wake up in the morning. I don't like talking on the phone much – I usually send text messages.

MIGUEL
I always have my phone with me – when I'm at home and when I'm at work, and I use it on the way to work to talk and check my emails. But I don't have it by the bed at night – I put it on "silent" and leave it in the kitchen. I want to sleep!

SAM
I use my phone all the time, but not at the movies, and not on a plane. I have it on at night by the bed. You never know – maybe someone needs to call you.

JENNY
My phone is usually off and I don't use it much. I use it to call people at the airport or on a bus – sometimes I need to say I'm late. But I don't like sending text messages.

a

b

1 READING

a Match the phrases in the box with pictures a–e.

at the movies   in bed   in the car
in a restaurant   on a mountain

b Look at pictures a–e again. Answer the questions.

1 What object is in all the pictures?
2 Which are … ?
- a good idea
- pretty normal
- a bad idea

c Read the message board comments and answer the questions.

1 You call the five people. They're in a restaurant. Who answers?
2 You call the five people at 3 a.m. Who answers?

d Which person do you think … ?

a has good ideas
b has a problem

e Write a comment about you and your phone for the message board.

f Read your comment to your partner. Are you the same?

2 VOCABULARY Place phrases with prepositions

a Find phrases in the message board with *in*, *on*, or *at* and the nouns in the box. Add them to the chart.

~~café~~   airport   car   work   bed   plane
movies   bus   restaurant   home

in		on	at	
in a café	______	______	______	______
______	______	______	______	______

b You're in a place in 2a and your partner calls you. Tell your partner what you're doing. Your partner guesses the place.

I'm going to work.

Are you in the car?

c Now go to Vocabulary Focus 10B on p. 147.

d Sound and spelling /ə/

1 10.09 Listen to the sound /ə/ in these words. Is it stressed or unstressed?
correct   idea   apartment   station

2 10.10 Listen to these words. Underline the /ə/ sound in each word.

about   banana   woman   television
problem   breakfast   company   information

3 Practice saying the words.

3 LISTENING AND GRAMMAR Present continuous: negative and questions

a 10.11 Listen and match conversations 1–5 with pictures a–e.

b Do you think … ?

1 Jack likes Ellie
2 Ellie likes Jack

How do you know?

c 10.12 Complete the chart. Listen and check.

+	–
I'm working.	I'm ______ ______.
I'm having dinner.	I'm ______ ______ dinner.

d 10.13 Complete Jack's questions. Listen and check.

1 **JACK** What ______ ______ doing?
ELLIE I'm at the bus stop. I'm going home.
2 **JACK** ______ ______ working?
ELLIE No, I'm not working.
3 **ELLIE** I'm watching a movie.
JACK Oh, what ______ ______ watching?

e 10.14 **Pronunciation** Listen to the questions in 3d again. Which word gets the most stress in each question?

f Now go to Grammar Focus 10B on p. 132.

g **Communication 10B** Student A go to p. 114. Student B go to p. 112.

4 SPEAKING

a You and a partner are in different places. You want to meet. Before you speak on the phone, write notes. Think about these questions:

- Where are you? (Choose a place from Vocabulary Focus 10B on page 147.)
- What are you doing? (Think of two or more activities.)
- When do you want to meet? (Think of a day, a time, and a place.)

b Call your partner and have a conversation.

- Ask where your partner is and what he/she is doing.
- Plan when and where to meet your partner.

Hi, Tom.
What are you doing?

I'm writing a report.

Are you free this evening? Do you want to go to Café Cabana?

10C EVERYDAY ENGLISH
What time's the train?

Learn to ask for travel information

- **P** Sound and spelling: /ɪə/ and /eə/
- **W** A text asking for information

1 LISTENING

a Look at pictures a and b and talk about the questions.

1 Where are Javier and Owen going?
2 Where do you think they go before?

b 10.18 Listen to Part 1. Check your ideas in 1a.

c 10.18 Listen to Part 1 again. Answer the questions.

1 What does Javier say about Jim?
2 Do they know what time the train leaves?

2 PRONUNCIATION Sound and spelling: /ɪə/ and /eə/

a 10.19 Listen to these words. Which word has a different sound?

here **yeah** **really**

b 10.20 Listen and complete the chart with the words in the box.

chair care year dear hair
near there clear pair zero

Sound 1 /ɪə/	Sound 2 /eə/
here	*yeah*

c 10.20 Listen again and repeat.

a

3 LISTENING

a Look at picture b. What questions does Owen ask the ticket agent at the train station?

b 10.21 Listen to Part 2. Check your ideas in 3a.

c 10.21 Listen to Part 2 again. Complete the information.

1 Time of next train: ______
2 Time now: ______
3 Platform: ______

d In your country, what is an easy way to travel – train, bus, car?

b

4 USEFUL LANGUAGE Asking for travel information

a Who says these expressions – a passenger (P) or the ticket agent (TA)?

1 The next train is at 2:15.
2 Which platform is it?
3 Excuse me.
4 The train leaves in ten minutes.
5 No, you change at Penn Station.
6 Yes? How can I help you?
7 What time's the next train to Philadelphia?
8 Is it a direct train?
9 It's Platform 4.

b 10.22 Listen and check your answers in 4a. Then listen again and repeat.

c 10.23 Complete the sentences with *at* or *in*. Listen and check.

1 The next train leaves ______ half an hour.
2 The next train leaves ______ five o'clock.

d 10.24 Put the conversation in the correct order. Then listen and check.

A
- ☐ So, at 5:15. And is it a direct bus?
- ☐ Great! Thanks for your help.
- ☐ What time's the next bus to Dallas?
- 1 Excuse me.
- ☐ OK, and which bus stop is it?

B
- ☐ The next bus leaves in 20 minutes.
- ☐ It's stop 7, near the ticket office.
- ☐ No problem.
- ☐ Yes? How can I help you?
- ☐ No, you change at Austin.

e Practice the conversation in 4d with a partner. Take turns being the ticket agent and the passenger. Change the times, kind of transportation, and the platforms / bus stops.

5 SPEAKING

Communication 10C

Student A go to p. 110.
Student B go to p. 112.

6 WRITING

a Owen helped his friend Anthony plan a vacation to Washington, D.C. Anthony sends Owen a message. Read it and answer the questions.

1 Where's Anthony now?
2 What two questions does he ask?

> Hi, Owen. I'm traveling to Washington, D.C. right now on the train. Sorry, I can't remember two things. First, where can I find a taxi at the train station? And how much is it from the station to the hotel?
> Thanks!
> Anthony

b Now go to Writing Plus 10C on p. 162 for Word order in questions.

c Write a message to a friend. Ask two questions in your message. Here are some ideas:

Hi …
I'm going / doing / having …
Sorry, I can't remember …
Where / How / When … ?
Thanks …

d Read another student's message. Try to answer the questions.

UNIT PROGRESS TEST

CHECK YOUR PROGRESS

YOU CAN NOW DO THE UNIT PROGRESS TEST.

UNIT 10
Review

1 GRAMMAR

a Correct the present continuous sentences.

> Carmen be wearing a yellow T-shirt.
Carmen's wearing a yellow T-shirt.

1 You wearing my shoes!
2 They're geting a taxi.
3 I'm writeing to Kelly.
4 The class starting.
5 She's haveing lunch.
6 We waiting.

b Write present continuous questions with the words and phrases.

1 where / you / sit ?
2 you / wear / black shoes ?
3 it / rain ?
4 you / use / a computer ?
5 why / you / study / English ?
6 what / your friends / do ?

c Ask and answer the questions in 1b.

d Complete the phone conversation with the verbs in parentheses.

GABY Hi, it's me.
JUAN Oh, hi. What [1]______ (you / do)?
GABY I [2]______ (talk) to you, of course. I'm on the train.
JUAN Oh, very funny. Well, I [3]______ (cook) dinner. So, [4]______ (you / listen to) music?
GABY Mm, no. I [5]______ (read) a book.
JUAN Oh, great. What's the weather like there?
GABY Not good. It [6]______ (rain) outside.
JUAN Well, it [7]______ (not / rain) here – it [8]______ (snow)! But Gwen and Carla are in the yard.
GABY The yard? Why? What [9]______ (they / do)?
JUAN They [10]______ (make) a snowman!

2 VOCABULARY

a Write the rooms.

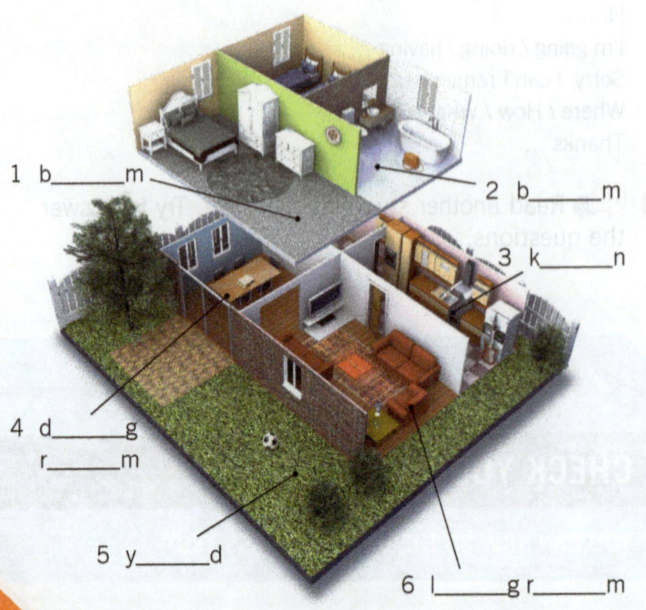

b Complete the questions with *in*, *on*, or *at*.

1 Do you listen to music ______ the car?
2 Do you sleep ______ trains / buses / planes?
3 Do you read ______ bed?
4 Do you eat ______ the movies?
5 Were you ______ home yesterday for lunch?
6 Did you play volleyball ______ school?
7 What's ______ the floor in this room?
8 Are there any pictures ______ the walls?

c Ask and answer the questions in 2b.

3 SOUND AND SPELLING

a Notice the two sounds and the letters in **bold**.

1 /tʃ/ **ch**oose
2 /θ/ **th**ree

b 10.25 Complete the chart with the words in the box. Practice saying the words.

ba**th**room bir**th**day **ch**ange **ch**oose
kit**ch**en ques**t**ion **th**anks **th**ree

/tʃ/	/θ/
choose	*three*

c 10.26 Are the two sounds in **bold** in each sentence the same (S) or different (D)? Practice saying the sentences.

1 The m**ea**l is h**ere**.
2 W**ear** a p**air** of shoes.
3 Th**eir** house is n**ear**.
4 It's r**ea**l h**air**.
5 Y**eah**, it's th**ere**.
6 Wh**ere**'s the ch**air**?

REVIEW YOUR PROGRESS

How well did you do in this unit? Write 3, 2, or 1 for each objective.
3 = very well 2 = well 1 = not so well

I CAN ...	
talk about my home	☐
ask where people are and what they're doing	☐
ask for travel information	☐

CAN DO OBJECTIVES

- Talk about people's lives
- Talk about things you know how to do
- Talk about opinions

UNIT 11

ACHIEVERS

GETTING STARTED

a Look at the picture and answer the questions.

1 What did this man do before he went into his tent? What are his plans tomorrow?

2 Check (✓) the things the man can do in his tent tonight. Why can't he do some things?

☐ listen to music ☐ cook dinner
☐ read a magazine ☐ do yoga
☐ play the guitar ☐ sleep well

3 What do you think he is writing in his book?

4 What questions do you want to ask him? Write down three.

b Would you like to be where this man is? Why / Why not?

11A SHE WENT AROUND THE EARTH

Learn to talk about people's lives

G Object pronouns

V Life events

1 READING

a Think of two famous people from your country (present or past). Ask and answer the questions with a partner.

1. Why are / were they famous?
2. What do you know about them?
3. Do you think people from other countries know about them? Why / Why not?

b Read *They Were the First!* Who ... ?

1. died over 15 years ago
2. had new ideas for computers
3. studied and worked at the same time
4. came from a poor family
5. lived in a few different places
6. had one child

c Read *They Were the First!* again. Choose one thing about each person you think is interesting and say why.

THEY WERE THE FIRST!

#1 THE FIRST WOMAN IN SPACE

Valentina Tereshkova (born 1937)

Who is she?

A Russian cosmonaut

What did she do?

In 1963, she flew in *Vostok 6*. She went around the Earth 48 times, and she was in space for almost three days.

Her life

She was born in 1937 in a small town in Russia. Her father was a tractor driver, and her mother worked in a factory. She finished school at 16 and started work in a factory. In her free time, she studied and she also went parachute jumping.

In 1963, she got married, and the next year she had a daughter, Elena. After that, Valentina never flew into space again.

2 VOCABULARY Life events

a 11.01 Look at these events in a person's life. Match events 1–6 with pictures a–f. Listen and check.

1. die
2. grow up
3. finish college
4. get married
5. go to school
6. be born

b Write the events in three lists.

1. everyone does this
2. most people do this
3. only some people do this

c Compare your lists with other students. Are they the same?

d Read *They Were the First!* again. Write simple past sentences about the years below.

Valentina Tereshkova
• 1937 • 1953 • 1963 • 1964

William Higinbotham
• 1910 • 1928 • 1932 • 1949

1937 – Valentina was born.

Language Plus Years

To say a year, we usually say the numbers in pairs:

1937 → 19 37 *nineteen thirty-seven* 2021 → 20 21 *twenty twenty-one*

We sometimes say the complete number for years after 2000:

2019 = *two thousand nineteen* 2021 = *two thousand twenty-one*

Note: 1900 = *nineteen hundred* 2000 = *two thousand*

2005 = *two thousand five*

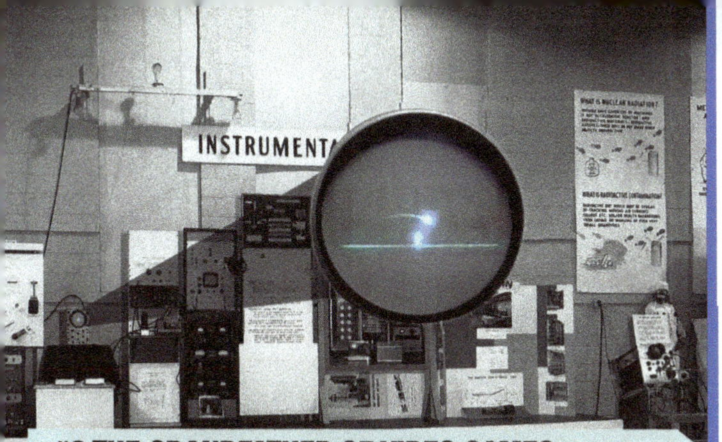

#2 THE GRANDFATHER OF VIDEO GAMES

William Higinbotham (1910–1994)

Who was he?

An American scientist

What did he do?

In 1958, he made a video game called "Tennis for Two." It was the first video game in the world, and people waited in line all day to play it.

His life

He was born in 1910, and he grew up in Caledonia, New York. When he was 18, he went to college, and four years later he studied at Cornell University.

When he was 39, he got married and moved to Bellport, New York, where he worked at a science lab. William wanted to make a fun game for people to play at his science lab, so he made "Tennis for Two," and he showed it during Visitor Day. It was a big success – but he didn't make any money from it!

e Sound and spelling Numbers

1 11.02 Listen to the words.
thirty thirteen
In each word ...
a Underline the main stress. Is it in the first part of the word or the second part?
b Does the letter *t* sound like /t/ or more like /d/?

2 11.03 Listen to eight numbers. Write the number you hear.

3 Work with a partner.
Student A: Say one of the numbers in the box.
Student B: Point to the number.
Then switch roles.

14	40	18	80	16	60	15	50	13	30

f Now go to Vocabulary Focus 11A on p. 154.

3 LISTENING AND GRAMMAR

Object pronouns

a 11.06 Listen to two friends talking about Valentina Tereshkova. Check (✓) the questions you can answer after listening to their conversation.

1 ☐ Where did she go to school?
2 ☐ Why did she get the job?
3 ☐ How did she meet her husband?
4 ☐ Where does she live now?
5 ☐ What does she want to do in the future?

b 11.06 Listen again and answer the questions you checked in 3a.

c 11.07 Complete the sentences from the conversation with the words in the box. Listen and check.

he	him	she	her

1 ______'s a Russian cosmonaut. Do you know about ______?
2 She married a cosmonaut. She met ______ in 1963. ______ was in the same space program.

d Underline the correct words to complete the rules.

1 We use **he** and **she** *before / after* a verb.
2 We use **him** and **her** *before / after* a verb or preposition.

e Now go to Grammar Focus 11A on p. 132.

4 SPEAKING

a Write four or five events in your life and the years.

2005–2019 – I lived in Panama City.
2019 – I started college.

b Work in pairs. Read your partner's sentences and ask some questions.

Where did you ...?
When did you ...?
Why did you ...?

c Tell the class two things about your partner's life.

11B SHE CAN PULL A PLANE

Learn to talk about things you know how to do

G *can* for ability

V Abilities

1 READING

a Look at 1–3 below. What's difficult for you to do? Why / Why not?

1 be cold for a long time
2 swim underwater
3 pull or carry big objects

b Read *Amazing Humans.* Are the amazing humans real or not?

c Read *Amazing Humans* again. Answer the questions.

1 How long can Wim Hof stay in a cold bath?
2 How long can the Bajau Laut people stay underwater?
3 How does Seema Bhadoria pull things?

d Which real person/people in *Amazing Humans* can do something useful?

2 GRAMMAR *can*: affirmative and negative

a Complete the chart. Check your answers in the text.

Affirmative			
I **can** You **can** He/She ______	swim underwater.	We **can** They ______	swim underwater.
Negative			
I **can't** You **can't** He/She ______	make ice.	We **can't** They ______	make ice.

b Underline examples of *can*/*can't* in *Amazing Humans.* What is after *can*/*can't*, a noun or a verb?

c Now go to Grammar Focus 11B Part 1 on p. 134.

AMAZING HUMANS

Do you sometimes do things that are different and interesting? Do you make videos of these things? Maybe you're not Superman or Superwoman, but you can do something amazing. Here are some stories about people who can do amazing things!

THE ICEMAN

Wim Hof is from the Netherlands, and he's often called "The Iceman." He can't make ice, but he can sit in a bath of ice for one hour, 52 minutes, and two seconds. He doesn't feel cold. In 2009, he ran more than 40 kilometers in –20°C wearing only shorts!

THE FISHMEN

The Bajau Laut people in Southeast Asia can swim underwater for a long time. Sometimes they can go underwater for more than five minutes. They can also see very well in the water – it helps them to see the fish!

THE STRONG WOMAN

Seema Bhadoria is an amazing young woman from India – she can pull really big objects with only her teeth. When she was only 18 years old, she pulled a plane with her teeth! She can also pull a ship or a big truck.

3 VOCABULARY Abilities

a Match the verbs in the box with pictures a–d.

cook sing swim paint

b Now go to Vocabulary Focus 11B on p. 155.

Language Plus (*very* / *pretty*) *well*

*I can swim **very well**.* = I'm very good.
*I can swim **well**.* = I'm good.
*I can swim **pretty well**.* = I'm OK.
*I **can't** swim **at all**.* = It's impossible for me.

c Talk about people you know and what they can or can't do.

My brother can't dance very well.

4 LISTENING

a Read the job description. Does the school want someone who can do one thing or a lot of things?

JOB ALERT CLOSE ⊗

We need people to work at our summer school in Chapel Hill.

We want people who can do a lot of different things – sing, dance, play the guitar, draw, ride a horse, but we also want good teachers!

If you're interested, please send us an email or give us a call …

b 11.12 Listen to Claire, the principal at the school, talk to Andy. Is he a good person for the job?

c 11.12 Listen again. What can Andy do? Complete sentences 1–4 with the words and phrases in the box.

teach ride a horse play the guitar sing dance

1 He can ______ and ______ pretty well.
2 He can ______ very well.
3 He can't ______ very well.
4 He can't ______ at all.

5 GRAMMAR *can*: questions

a 11.13 Complete the conversations. Listen and check your answers.

1 **CLAIRE** And ______ ______ sing?
ANDY Yes, ______ ______.
2 **CLAIRE** ______ ______ dance well?
ANDY No, ______ ______.

b Now go to Grammar Focus 11B Part 2 on p. 134.

c 11.15 **Pronunciation** Listen to the sentences. Check (✓) when *can*/*can't* is stressed.

1 ☐ I can sing pretty well.
2 ☐ I can't dance very well.
3 ☐ Can you sing?
4 ☐ Yes, I can.

d Practice saying the sentences. Underline the correct words to complete the rules.

Can *is / isn't* stressed in affirmative sentences and questions.
Can *is / isn't* stressed in negative sentences and short answers.

e 11.16 Complete the conversation with the correct form of *can*. Listen and check.

A ______ Andy play the guitar?
B Yes, he ______.
A And ______ he ride a horse?
B Yes, he ______ ride a horse very well.
A ______ he teach?
B No, he ______ teach at all.

f Practice the conversation in 5e with a partner.

6 SPEAKING

a Work in pairs. Write one question with *can* for each topic.

- sports — *Can you play tennis?*
- food — *Can you make a cake?*
- language
- music / art

b Work with a new partner. Ask and answer your questions in 6a.

Can you play tennis?

No, I can't play tennis at all.

c Work with your first partner again. Tell them about your second partner.

Lola can speak Portuguese pretty well, but she can't speak Italian.

11C EVERYDAY ENGLISH
What do you think?

Learn to talk about opinions

P Consonant clusters

W An email to a friend

1 LISTENING

a Ask and answer the questions.

1 What's your favorite restaurant in your town or city?
2 What food do you usually eat there?

b Look at pictures a–c. What do you think happens in the story, idea 1 or 2?

1 Leah and Carter are brother and sister. They're at a restaurant. Their mom calls and invites them for dinner. They leave the restaurant and go to her house.
2 Carter and Leah are brother and sister. They're at a restaurant. They talk about what restaurants their mom would like. They can't decide what restaurant to take her to.

c 11.17 Listen. Check your answer in 1b.

d 11.17 Listen again. Read the sentences. Write Leah (L), Carter (C), or both (B). Who ... ?

1 loves Indian food
2 talked to their mom on the phone
3 wants to visit their mom next weekend
4 wants to take their mom to an Indian restaurant
5 doesn't think an Italian restaurant is a good idea for their mom
6 is hungry

e Are there any interesting places to visit in/near your town or city?

2 USEFUL LANGUAGE Talking about opinions

a Look at the expressions. Do we use them to ... ?

a ask for an opinion
b give an opinion
c have the same opinion
d have a different opinion

1 Where's a good place to take Mom?
2 No, that's not my favorite.
3 Maybe you're right.
4 I don't think the Italian place is a good idea.
5 It looks good.
6 How about that new restaurant near here?
7 I think you're right.
8 What do you think?

11.18 Listen and check your answers.

b 11.18 **Pronunciation** Listen to sentences 1–8 in 2a again. Underline the words with the most stress. Listen again and repeat.

c 11.19 Look at expressions 1–4. Are they in group a, b, c, or d in 2a? Listen and check.

1 Me, too.
2 What's good here?
3 What about the Italian restaurant near you?
4 I'm not so sure.

d 11.20 Put the words in the correct order to make expressions. Listen and check.

1 visit her / we can go / next weekend .
2 you think / what do / new restaurant / of the ?
3 you're / I think / right .
4 so / think / I don't .
5 idea / good / that's / a .

e Complete the conversation with your ideas.

A What do you think of English?
YOU ______
A Yes, maybe you're right. What about the grammar?
YOU ______
A Really? I don't think so. I think your language is very hard.
YOU ______
A Well, all languages are a little hard.
YOU ______

f Practice the conversation in 2e with a partner. Take turns being A.

3 PRONUNCIATION Consonant clusters

a 11.21 Listen to the words. Notice how the letters in **bold** are pronounced. Listen again and repeat.

1 /t/ righ**t** 2 /ŋk/ thi**nk** 3 /st/ touri**st**

b 11.22 Listen and match the letters in **bold** in 1–6 with a–f.

1 a**sk**	3 fi**nd**	5 restaura**nt**
2 da**nce**	4 difficu**lt**	6 si**x**
a /nt/	c /sk/	e /nd/
b /lt/	d /ks/	f /ns/

c Practice saying the words.

4 SPEAKING

Communication 11C

Student A go to p. 113.
Student B go to p. 114.

5 WRITING

a Read Leah's email to an old friend. What does she like about her life in Ann Arbor?

Ann Arbor

Hi Hailey,

Thanks for your email – it was really good to hear from you.

Things here at school are going well. Ann Arbor is a great city, and there are a lot of things I can do. I'm making some new friends in my classes. I study with a girl named Megan. She's from Ann Arbor, and she's really nice. She and her boyfriend, Chris, helped me a lot when I arrived. I often see them at the library. I also know my brother, of course! He's really busy with school and work, but we sometimes meet for coffee or dinner. It's good to have him in the same city.

My apartment is pretty small, but it's comfortable. I live with three other girls, but we have a good time. It's near my classes, so I can walk to class every day. I like that!

I miss my friends from home. How are things at school for you?

Write again soon.

Love,

Leah

b Now go to Writing Plus 11C on p. 163 for Pronouns.

c Write an email to a friend. Tell them about your life now. Here are some ideas:

- Say hi and thank the person for his/her email. (*Hi … Thanks …*)
- Write about your life – your job or studies. (*I'm working/studying …*)
- Write about family and/or friends. (*My parents are well … I see my friend Luisa every …*)
- Say goodbye and ask the person to write to you. (*Goodbye for now … Love / See you soon …*)

d Read another student's email. What's interesting about their life?

UNIT PROGRESS TEST

CHECK YOUR PROGRESS

YOU CAN NOW DO THE UNIT PROGRESS TEST.

UNIT 11
Review

1 GRAMMAR

a Complete the sentences with the correct pronoun.

1 I like Rob, but I don't think he likes ______.
2 Those shoes are beautiful. Can I buy ______, please?
3 Sarah's a good friend. I met ______ at college.
4 My husband and I live in the city, but my parents live in a small town. They sometimes visit ______ on weekends.
5 They had a baby boy, and they named ______ Antonio.
6 Happy birthday! I got ______ a present!
7 Your car is dirty. You need to clean ______.

b Look at the chart. Then complete the conversation with the words and phrases in the box.

	dance	play tennis	ride a horse
Beto	✗	✓✓	✓
Melanie	✓	✗	✓✓

can (x4) can't can she can you
he can't I can she can

A [1]______ Beto dance?
B No, [2]______ . But he [3]______ play tennis very well, and he [4]______ ride a horse.
A What about Melanie? [5]______ ride a horse?
B Yes, [6]______. She can ride a horse very well, and she [7]______ dance, but she [8]______ play tennis.
A What about you? [9]______ play tennis?
B Yes, [10]______ .

c Ask a partner about the activities in 1b. Use *Can you ... ?*

2 VOCABULARY

a Complete the text with the correct form of the verb phrases in the box.

have a baby boy finish school be born
go to college die grow up get married

My parents met in London, and I [1]______ in England, but my family came here to Michigan when I was three. I [2]______ here, and I don't remember anything about England. I [3]______ when I was eighteen. I got a job at a hotel, but it wasn't very interesting.
Then I [4]______ in Atlanta. I studied engineering, and I met Daniela – she's now my wife!
Daniela and I [5]______ five years ago. We both got good jobs in Atlanta, but then my father [6]______, so we came back here to Michigan to be near my mom.
We [7]______ last year. Life is good!

b Complete the verb phrases with the words in the box.

dinner basketball a motorcycle songs to work walls

play	cards, [1]__________, volleyball
sing	[2]__________
paint	a picture, [3]__________
ride	a horse, [4]__________, a bike
drive	a car, [5]__________
cook	[6]__________

c Which of the things in 2b do you do every day? Which do you sometimes do? Which do you never do?

3 SOUND AND SPELLING

a 11.23 Underline the main stress in these words. Practice saying the words.

thirteen	nineteen
fifteen	twenty
sixty	fourteen
forty	seventy
ninety	thirty
eighteen	eighty

b 11.24 Are the sounds in **bold** the same (S) or different (D)? Practice saying the words.

1 si**x** – than**ks**
2 d**a**nce – **a**nswer
3 **r**ight – **wh**ite
4 touri**st** – dan**ced**
5 **a**sk – **sch**ool
6 s**i**ng – s**a**ng

REVIEW YOUR PROGRESS

How well did you do in this unit? Write 3, 2, or 1 for each objective.
3 = very well 2 = well 1 = not so well

I CAN ...	
talk about people's lives	☐
talk about things I know how to do	☐
talk about opinions	☐

CAN DO OBJECTIVES

- Talk about future plans
- Ask and answer about future plans
- Make and accept invitations

UNIT 12

PLANS

GETTING STARTED

a Look at the picture and answer the questions.

1 Do you think this family is going to … ?
- go on a long or short vacation
- go somewhere near or far
- go somewhere hot or cold
- go by car or drive to the airport

Why?

2 What did the man do … ?
- the day before the trip
- the morning of the trip
- a month before the trip

3 What do you think this family is going to do on the trip? Why?

b Talk about the questions.

1 When you go on vacation, do you pack too much or not enough?
2 What do you sometimes forget to take when you go on vacation?

12A I'M GOING TO TAKE A LONG HOT BATH

Learn to talk about future plans

- **G** *be going to*: affirmative and negative
- **V** Months and future time expressions; Ordinal numbers

1 READING

a Talk about everyday objects and activities that are important to you. Think about:

- food and drink (*my morning coffee* …)
- your things (*my sofa* …)
- things you do (*listen to music* …)

> Every day I play video games – I really like them.

b Read about *Danger Zone*. Is it about … ?

1 a fun vacation   2 a dangerous competition

c Read about the TV show again. Answer the questions.

1 Where do people on the TV show go?
2 Do they have an easy time? Why / Why not?
3 What do the two best people get?

d Read the people's ideas for after the TV show. Which is the best idea? Tell a partner.

2 GRAMMAR *be going to*: affirmative

a 12.01 Complete Mason's sentences with the words in the box. Listen and check.

to	are	going

1 I'm _________ to sleep for a long time.
2 Abby's going _________ take a long hot bath.
3 Santiago and Manuela _________ going to have their favorite food and drink.

b Underline the correct answer in the rule.

> We use *be* + *going to* to talk about *now* / *the future*.

c 12.01 **Pronunciation** Listen to the sentences in 2a again. Notice the sentence stress and the pronunciation of *going to*. Answer the questions.

1 Do we stress *going*, the main verb, or both?
2 Can we hear the words *going to* clearly?

Practice saying the sentences.

d Now go to Grammar Focus 12A Part 1 on p. 134.

e Write three sentences about something you're going to do after class.

After class, I'm going to meet my friend Diego.

f Tell other students your sentences in 2e.

> I'm going to study in the Learning Center. What about you?

> I'm going to get some coffee.

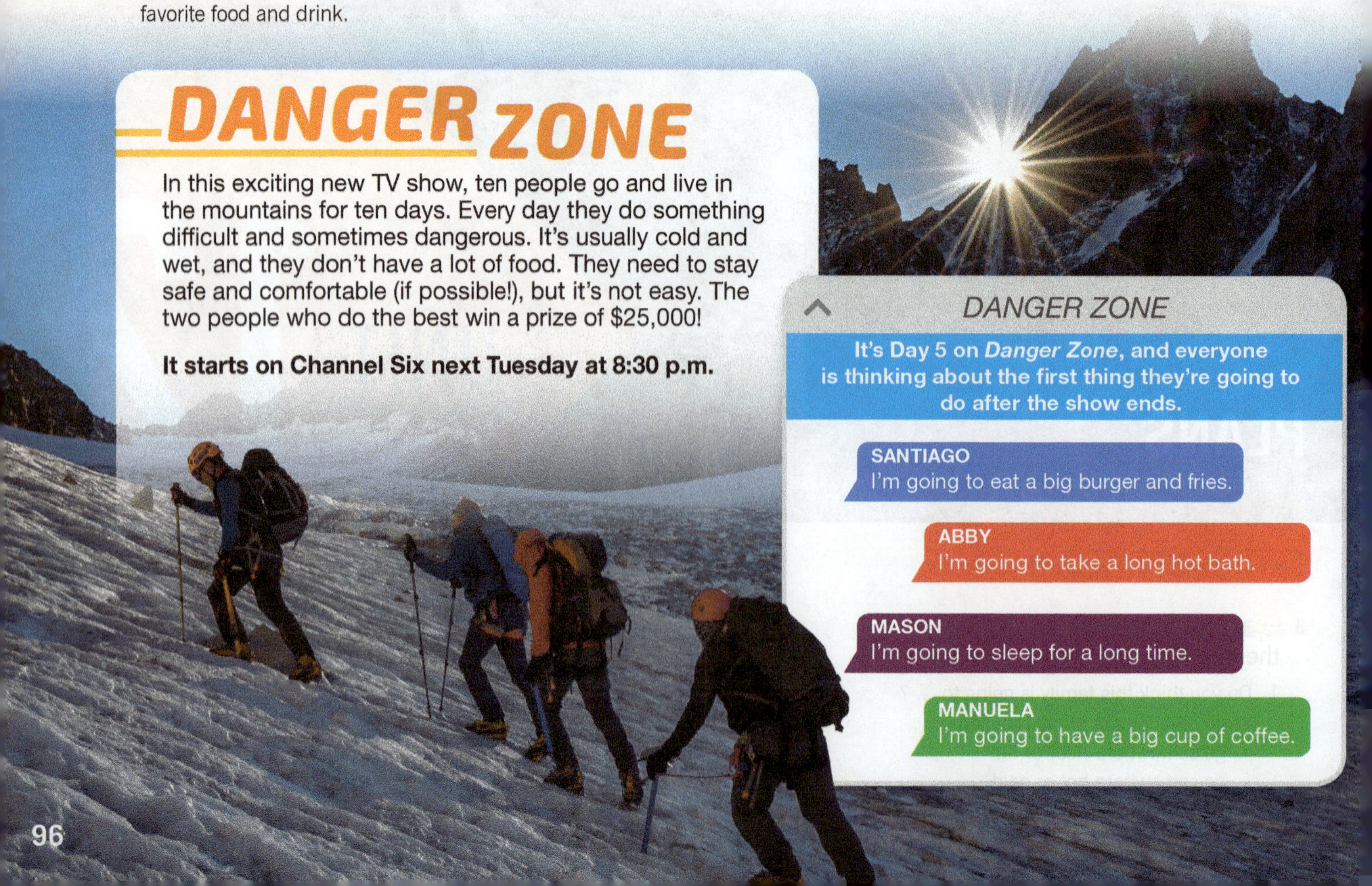

DANGER ZONE

In this exciting new TV show, ten people go and live in the mountains for ten days. Every day they do something difficult and sometimes dangerous. It's usually cold and wet, and they don't have a lot of food. They need to stay safe and comfortable (if possible!), but it's not easy. The two people who do the best win a prize of $25,000!

It starts on Channel Six next Tuesday at 8:30 p.m.

DANGER ZONE

It's Day 5 on *Danger Zone*, and everyone is thinking about the first thing they're going to do after the show ends.

SANTIAGO
I'm going to eat a big burger and fries.

ABBY
I'm going to take a long hot bath.

MASON
I'm going to sleep for a long time.

MANUELA
I'm going to have a big cup of coffee.

3 VOCABULARY Months and future time expressions; Ordinal numbers

a It's Monday morning. Put time expressions 1–6 in the correct place on the timeline.

1 tonight 2 tomorrow 3 this Wednesday 4 on Friday 5 on the weekend 6 next Monday

MONDAY		TUESDAY		WEDNESDAY		THURSDAY		FRIDAY		SATURDAY		SUNDAY		MONDAY	
a.m.	p.m.	a.m.	p.m.	a.m.	p.m.	a.m.	p.m.	a.m.	p.m.	a.m.	p.m.	a.m.	p.m.	a.m.	p.m.

Language Plus The date

*What's the date today? It's **August fifth**.*
*When's your birthday? It's **on March twentieth**.*
Note: With dates we use ordinal numbers:
first, second, third, fourth …

b Now go to Vocabulary Focus 12A on p. 156.

c Ask and answer the questions with a partner. Use time expressions in your answers.

1 When's your next English class?
2 When's your next English test?
3 When's your birthday?

It's on November fifteenth.

4 LISTENING

a 12.06 Listen to Paola (P), Azra (A), and Gabe (G) talk about their vacation plans this summer. Match them with pictures a–c.

b 12.06 Listen again. Are the sentences true or false?

1 Paola often goes to a cooking school for vacation.
2 The trip to Italy is a different kind of vacation for Azra.
3 Gabe doesn't want to make money on the farm.

c Which vacation plan do you like? Which don't you like? Why?

a

b

c

5 GRAMMAR *be going to*: negative

a 12.07 Listen and complete the sentences.

1 **PAOLA** I ______ going ______ have a normal vacation.
2 **AZRA** We ______ going ______ do that this year.

b Now go to Grammar Focus 12A Part 2 on p. 134.

c 12.09 Complete the conversations. Listen and check.

1 **A** After class, I'______ not ______ to do my homework.
B Why not?
A I'm tired. I'm going ______ do it tomorrow.
2 **C** After class, I'______ not ______ to go home.
D Why not?
C I'm going ______ meet friends at a café.

d Practice the conversations in 5c. Use your own ideas to have similar conversations.

6 SPEAKING

a Write two things you're going to do on your next vacation. Think about:

- places
- things to buy
- activities
- sports
- places to stay
- people

b Write two things from your everyday life you aren't going to do on your vacation.

- things you do at school / work
- things you do at home

c Talk to other students about your ideas in 6a and 6b. Do you all have the same ideas?

I'm going to go to the beach.

I'm not going to read work emails.

12B WHAT ARE YOU GOING TO DO THIS WEEKEND?

Learn to ask and answer about future plans

- **G** *be going to:* questions
- **V** Common verbs and collocations

ONLY 4,000 WEEKENDS IN YOUR LIFE!
So, What Are You Going To Do With Them?

What's your answer to this question? Perhaps it's "I don't know" or "Not a lot." In her new book, *What the Most Successful People Do on the Weekend*, Laura Vanderkam says these are bad answers. She says the weekend is a time to relax, but also a time to do interesting things. With only 4,000 weekends in our life, each one is important. So don't just sit on the sofa and watch TV. It's a good idea to plan the weekend – then you can use the time well. Here are some of her ideas:

1 Plan three to five activities to do on the weekend and write them down. Be sure you do these things.
2 Plan to read a book. Buy a book for the weekend and then plan a time to read it.
3 Write a list of 100 "big" things you'd like to do in your life. Choose one to do this weekend.
4 Get up early. Between 6:00 and 8:00 in the morning is the best time to do things. Plan to wake up early and do something before breakfast!
5 Turn off your phone and don't use your computer. You can read your emails on Monday. On Sunday evening, go for a run, play some music, or do yoga so you relax and don't think about work.
6 Don't clean your house or apartment on the weekend. It's a time to do things you like!

1 READING

a Talk about sentences 1–3 in small groups. Which are true for you?

1 Weekends are too short, and we don't have many of them.
2 It's not a good idea to do a lot on the weekend.
3 It's important to use the time well on the weekend.

b Read about Laura Vanderkam's new book. Which sentence in 1a is her main idea?

c Look at pictures a–e. Which does Laura say are good things to do on the weekend? Which aren't good?

d Look at Wendy's, David's, and Rachel's plans for the weekend. Match them with ideas 1–3 in the text.

e What do you think of Laura's ideas? Which do you like? Which don't you like? Why / Why not?

Great ideas! I'd like to try them.

That's not my idea of a good weekend.

Interesting ideas, but …

Wendy's big ideas

I'd like to …
- make a cheesecake
- visit Paris
- paint my room
- learn Chinese
- read a book by Stephen King
- start a blog
- go skydiving

DAVID'S SCHEDULE

	SUNDAY
10:00	
11:00	
12:00	Sit in the park and read my new book.
1:00	
2:00	Play basketball with friends.

Rachel's weekend to-do list

This weekend I'm going to:
1 go for a long run (10 km or more!).
2 invite some friends for dinner.
3 take my first tennis lesson.

2 VOCABULARY Common verbs and collocations

a 12.10 Match the verbs in the box with the words and phrases in 1–8. Listen and check.

paint clean use make invite visit go do play

1 ________ laundry / your homework
2 ________ someone to a party
3 ________ a friend
4 ________ a list / lunch
5 ________ a picture / a wall
6 ________ your apartment / your windows
7 ________ your phone / the Internet
8 ________ for a walk / shopping / to a museum
9 ________ sports

b Find examples of each verb on page 98. Add them to 1–9 in 2a.

c Tell a partner which activities in 2a and 2b you do on the weekend.

I always … I often …
I sometimes … I never …

d Now go to Vocabulary Focus 12B on p. 157.

e **Sound and spelling** /v/ and /w/

1 12.12 Listen and practice these sounds.
1 /v/ **v**isit 2 /w/ **w**eekend

2 12.13 Listen to these words and practice saying them.

in**v**ite **v**erb **w**atch **w**ith e**v**ening **w**ell ne**v**er

3 LISTENING AND GRAMMAR *be going to*: questions

a 12.14 Listen to Lee and Marcus talk to a friend about their weekend plans. Write their names on the line.

NO PLAN ⟷ CLEAR PLAN

b 12.14 Listen again. Check (✓) the things you know after listening to the conversations.

1 ☐ the name of the movie Lee's going to see
2 ☐ Lee's plans for Sunday
3 ☐ Marcus's shopping plans
4 ☐ the name of the restaurant Marcus is going to go to
5 ☐ Marcus's plans for Sunday

c 12.15 Check (✓) the correct questions in 1–2. Listen and check.

1 a ☐ What are you going to do on Saturday?
b ☐ What you are going to do on Saturday?
2 a ☐ You going to go shopping?
b ☐ Are you going to go shopping?

d Now go to Grammar Focus 12B on p. 134.

e 12.18 Put the words in the correct order to make questions. Listen and check.

1 what / you / this weekend / do / going to / are ?
2 go out / you / are / going to ?
3 what / going to / movie / see / are / you ?
4 you / are / buy / going to / what ?
5 go / going to / where / you / are ?

f Have two conversations with a partner.

1 Student A: You're Lee.
Student B: Ask questions 1, 2, and 3 in 3e.
2 Student B: You're Marcus.
Student A: Ask questions 1, 4, and 5 in 3e.

4 SPEAKING

a Write questions to ask your partner about their plans. Use the ideas below and *be going to*.

- this evening
- the weekend
- on your next birthday

b Ask your partner your questions in 4a. Listen to the answers and write your partner's name on the line in 3a.

c Compare your line with other students. Who has clear plans for the future?

12C EVERYDAY ENGLISH

Do you want to watch the game?

Learn to make and accept invitations

- P Sound and spelling: *oo*
- W An invitation

1 LISTENING

a You invite friends to your house. Which of these things do you do? Write *Yes*, *No*, or *Sometimes*.

- make special food
- do homework
- play video games
- cook with your friends
- listen to music
- watch a show or movie

b Talk about your ideas in 1a with a partner.

c Look at pictures a and b. What do you think Ryan invites Carlos to do?

d 12.19 Listen to Part 1. Check your answer in 1c.

e 12.19 Listen to Part 1 again. Underline the correct answer.

1 Carlos invites Ryan to *the movies / watch a football game*.
2 Ryan *has / doesn't have* plans for tonight.
3 Carlos *accepts / doesn't accept* Ryan's invitation.

2 USEFUL LANGUAGE Making and accepting invitations

a Look at the expressions. Do we use them to ... ?

a make an invitation
b accept an invitation
c say no to an invitation

1 Do you want to go see a movie?
2 I'd like to, but ...
3 OK, sure. That sounds like fun.
4 Are you free tonight?
5 Sorry. Next time!
6 Great. See you then!

12.20 Listen and check your answers.

b 12.21 Complete the conversation with the words in the box. Listen and check.

sorry	thank	love	want	OK	free	busy

A Do you [1]______ to go to dinner?
B Yes, I'd [2]______ to. [3]______ you.
A Are you [4]______ on Saturday?
B No, [5]______, I'm [6]______ on Saturday. But Sunday's [7]______.
A OK, we can go on Sunday.

c Practice the conversation in 2b with a partner.

3 LISTENING

a Do you often meet people from other countries? Where do you meet them?

b 12.22 Listen to Part 2. Answer the questions.

1 Where do they watch the game?
2 When did Carlos move there?

c 12.22 Listen to Part 2 again. Check (✓) the correct answers.

1 ☐ Carlos meets Ryan's friends for the first time.
2 ☐ Carlos knows Ryan's friends from before.
3 ☐ The football game is going to start soon.
4 ☐ The football game started before Carlos arrived.
5 ☐ Carlos doesn't understand football.
6 ☐ Carlos understands football.

d Why was Carlos confused about the football game?

4 PRONUNCIATION Sound and spelling: *oo*

a 12.23 Listen to these sentences. Notice the different *oo* sounds.

1 G**oo**d – now you're both here.
2 I'll bring the f**oo**d.

b 12.24 Listen to these words. Put them in the correct place in the chart.

cool cook spoon look
book soon football

Sound 1 /ʊ/	Sound 2 /uː/
good	*food*

c Practice saying the words in 2b with a partner.

5 SPEAKING

Communication 12C
Student A go to p. 110.
Student B go to p. 115.

6 WRITING

a Carlos wrote invitations to his new friends. Read the invitations and the replies. Do they say yes or no? Why?

Birthday on Saturday

Hi guys,

It's my birthday on Saturday. Do you want to come to my party?

It's at my apartment at 2:00. We're going to watch my favorite soccer team play on TV at 3:00.

I hope to see you then!

Carlos

RE: Birthday on Saturday

Hi Carlos,

Thanks for the invitation!

Sorry, but I'm working until 4:00 on Saturday. I can come late at 4:30. Is that OK with you? Maybe I can still see part of the soccer game!

Ryan

RE: Birthday on Saturday

Hi Carlos,

I'd love to come, but I'm at my parents' house until Sunday.

Do you want to watch a game next week? I'm free after 2:00. Soccer or football sounds good to me!

Hope you have a great time!

Steve

RE: Birthday on Saturday

Hi Carlos,

Thanks for the invitation. Adriana and I can come! What can we bring? We can make some cookies if you'd like!

See you Saturday!

Hayley

b Now go to Writing Plus 12C on p. 163 for Paragraphs.

c You want to meet a friend. Think of a place and time. Write an invitation. Here are some ideas:

Do you want to … ?
I'm free at …
See you …
We could …
Is that OK with you?

d Read another student's invitation. Write a reply.

UNIT PROGRESS TEST

CHECK YOUR PROGRESS

YOU CAN NOW DO THE UNIT PROGRESS TEST.

UNIT 12
Review

1 GRAMMAR

a Complete Emily's email with *be going to* and the verbs in parentheses.

> Hi Mia,
>
> I have so many plans for this week! This afternoon I [1]__________ (study), and then I [2]__________ (work) from Tuesday to Thursday. On Wednesday evening, I [3]__________ (cook) for my parents, and then on Thursday evening, Marco [4]__________ (cook) dinner for me!
>
> I [5]__________ (not / work) on Friday morning because you [6]__________ (arrive) at lunchtime! James [7]__________ (have) a party on Friday evening. Do you want to go? He [8]__________ (not / invite) a lot of people.
>
> It's a busy week for me! So I [9]__________ (not / do) any work or housework this weekend, and we [10]__________ (not / go) to a lot of different places! I hope that's OK.
>
> See you on Friday!
>
> Emily

b Correct the sentences.

\> "Is your friend going to have lunch with us?" "No, she not."
No, she's not.

1 "You are going to watch TV this evening?" "No, I'm not."
2 Are your mom going to cook your dinner this evening?
3 "Are you going to clean your bedroom?" "Yes, I'm going."
4 What do you going to wear tomorrow?
5 "Are your friends going to visit you today?" "Yes, they're."
6 What you going to do next summer?

c Ask and answer the questions in 1b. Use *be going to*.

2 VOCABULARY

a ~~Cross out~~ the answers that are NOT possible.

1 *tomorrow / on tomorrow*
2 *this / in / next / on* Friday
3 *on / in* the weekend
4 *on / this / in / next* June
5 *next / at* weekend
6 *on / in* Sunday
7 *in / on* three weeks
8 *this / at* afternoon

b Complete the ordinal numbers.

\> 6th s *i* *x* *t* h
1 2nd s _ _ _ _ d
2 30th t _ _ _ _ _ _ _ _ h
3 21st t _ _ _ _ _ y-f _ _ _ t
4 3rd t _ _ _ d
5 15th f _ _ _ _ _ _ _ _ h
6 9th n _ _ _ h

c Complete the questions with the words in the box.

clean play invite make use go

1 Do you often ______ to museums?
2 Are you going to ______ a cake this weekend?
3 Did you ______ any sports yesterday?
4 Are you going to ______ your bedroom today?
5 Do you ______ your computer every day?
6 Are you going to ______ someone for lunch next week?

d Ask and answer the questions in 2c.

3 SOUND AND SPELLING

a 12.25 Circle the /v/ sounds in the phrases and underline the /w/ sounds. Practice saying the phrases and sentences.

1 visit in the evening
2 We never invite Wendy.
3 I love weekends in the winter.
4 win video games every week
5 watch TV with Valeria and William
6 on Wednesday, November twelfth

b 12.26 Complete the chart with the words in the box. Practice saying the words.

good book football boots
cool look school soon

/ʊ/	/u/
cooking	*spoon*

REVIEW YOUR PROGRESS

How well did you do in this unit? Write 3, 2, or 1 for each objective.
3 = very well 2 = well 1 = not so well

I CAN ...	
talk about future plans	☐
ask and answer about future plans	☐
make and accept invitations	☐

Phonemic symbols

Vowel sounds

/ə/	/æ/	/ʊ/	/ɑ/	/ɪ/	/i/	/e/	/ʌ/	/ɜ/	/u/	/ɔ/
breakfast	man	put	got	chip	happy	men	up	shirt	who	walk

Diphthongs (two vowel sounds)

/eə/	/ɪə/	/ɔɪ/	/ɑɪ/	/eɪ/	/oʊ/	/ɑʊ/
hair	near	boy	nine	eight	window	now

Consonants

/p/ picnic	/b/ book	/f/ face	/v/ very	/t/ time	/d/ dog	/k/ cold	/g/ go
/θ/ think	/ð/ the	/tʃ/ chair	/dʒ/ job	/s/ sea	/z/ zoo	/ʃ/ shoe	/ʒ/ television
/m/ me	/n/ now	/ŋ/ sing	/h/ hot	/l/ late	/r/ red	/w/ went	/j/ yes

Irregular verbs

Infinitive	Simple past
be	was
begin	began
buy	bought
catch	caught
choose	chose
come	came
do	did
drink	drank
drive	drove
eat	ate
feel	felt
find	found
fly	flew
forget	forgot
get	got
give	gave
go	went
grow up	grew up
have	had
hear	heard
know	knew
leave	left
lose	lost

Infinitive	Simple past
meet	met
pay	paid
put	put
read	read
ride	rode
run	ran
say	said
see	saw
sell	sold
send	sent
sing	sang
sit	sat
sleep	slept
speak	spoke
swim	swam
take	took
teach	taught
tell	told
think	thought
understand	understood
wake up	woke up
wear	wore
write	wrote

COMMUNICATION PLUS

7B STUDENT A

a Look at picture 1. Write notes about their clothes.

b Tell Student B about the clothes the people in picture 1 are wearing. Find out their names and write them under each picture.

This person has a blouse and a skirt. What's this person's name?

c Listen to Student B talk about the clothes in picture 2. Tell him/her the people's names.

d Now go back to p. 58.

9A STUDENT B

a Read notes about your trip to Dubai, in the UAE. Make sentences from the notes. Use the simple past.

- in the north of the UAE
- plane to Dubai …
- didn't stay in a hotel …
- … my brother's apartment (he lives in Dubai)
- … then taxi around the city
- a lot of photos
- shopping – a lot of clothes
- restaurants – very good food

b Listen to Student A talk about a trip to Seville.

c Tell Student A about your trip. Find four things you both did on your trips.

12C STUDENT A

a You want to invite Student B to:

1 go for a walk this weekend.
2 meet for coffee.

Think about what you want to say. Start the conversation with Student B. Try to find times when you're both free.

Do you want to go for a walk this weekend?

YOUR SCHEDULE

SUN	visiting parents 12:00–5:00	THURS	work 8:00–6:00
MON	work 8:00–6:00	FRI	work 8:00–6:00 yoga 7:00–8:30
TUES	work 8:00–6:00	SAT	concert 7:00 p.m.
WED			

b Now go back to p. 101.

10C STUDENT A

a **Conversation 1.** Read your first card. Think about what you want to say. Then start the conversation with Student B with *Excuse me.*

1 You want to go to Chicago.
- Time now: 11:15 a.m.
- Ask about the next train.
- Ask about the platform.
- You have a big suitcase – it's difficult to run.

b **Conversation 2.** Now read your second card. Think about what you want to say. Listen to Student B and reply.

2 You're a ticket agent at a bus station.
- Time now: 2:45 p.m.

	Time	Bus stop	Price
Phoenix	3:00 p.m.	4	$16
Phoenix	4:00 p.m.	3	$11

c Now go back to p. 85.

7A STUDENT B

a You have a stall at a flea market. You sell the objects in the box.

pictures   clocks   lamps   chairs   old books

Write a price for each object.

b At Student A's stall, you see three things you like:

- some beautiful plates
- an interesting plant
- a good knife for your kitchen

Try to buy them for a good price.

They're expensive. Is $2 OK?

c Try to sell things to Student A.

They're $10 each. They're very old.

It's only $5 – it's very cheap.

8A STUDENT B

a Answer Student A's questions about Morgan.

1 year ago	**last weekend**	**on Monday**
in Atlanta, Georgia	at a party at her home	in class

b Ask Student C about Marcella.

Where was she a year ago?

Where was she last weekend?

Was she at work on Monday?

c Listen to Students A and C talk about Jaime.

d What is the same for all three people?

7C STUDENT A

a **Conversation 1.** You're a sales assistant at a store. Student B is your customer. You have six glasses, and they are $2.00 each. Your customer can pay by card. Start a conversation with *Hello, can I help you?*

b **Conversation 2.** You're a customer at a store. Student B is a sales assistant. You want to buy four plates. Ask how much they are.

c Now go back to p. 61.

8B STUDENT B

a Look at the pictures of Charlotte's day yesterday. Write notes about what she did.

b Listen to Student A talk about what Leo did yesterday.

c Tell Student A what Charlotte did yesterday. What activities are the same?

9B STUDENT A

a Read the information about the weather in Mumbai, in India. Listen to Student B and reply.

Weather in Mumbai	
Yesterday	hot, sunny
Today	cloudy, warm
Summer	a lot of rain, hot

b Ask Student B these questions about the weather in Berlin, in Germany.

What was the weather like yesterday?

What's the weather like today?

What's the weather like in winter?

c Now go back to p. 75.

10A STUDENT B

a Listen to Student A. Are they talking about picture 1, 2, or 3?

b Carlos is in picture 6. Tell Student A:

- where he is (*He's sitting in …*)
- what's in the next room (*There's a … next door.*)
- what he's doing (*He's …*)

c Listen to Student A again. Which picture are they talking about now?

d Choose picture 1 or 3. Describe it to Student A.

10B STUDENT B

a Look at the picture. What are the people doing? Write notes.

b Student A has a similar picture. Ask and answer questions to find five differences. Student A starts.

Is Ali in the kitchen?

Yes, he is.

Is he eating?

No, he's not. He's …

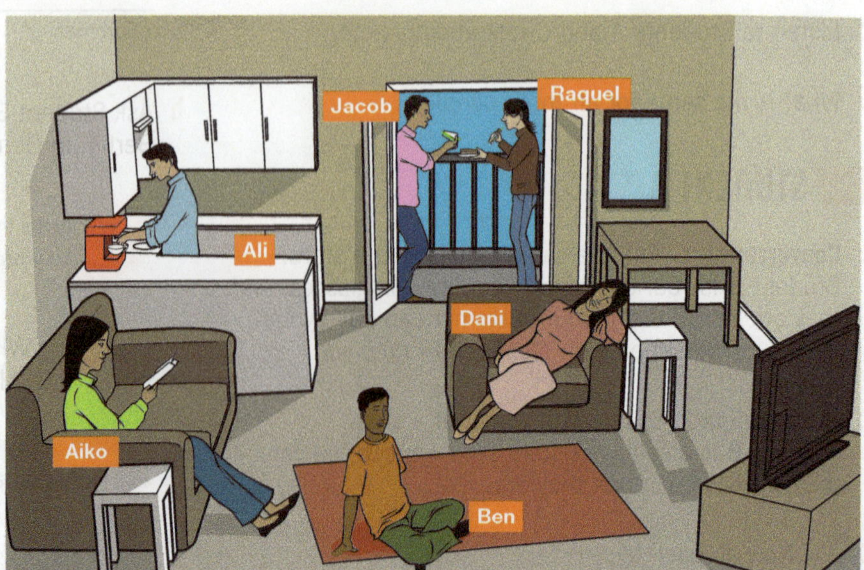

c ⋙ Now go back to p. 83.

7C STUDENT B

a **Conversation 1.** You're a customer at a store. Student A is a sales assistant. You want to buy four glasses. Ask how much they are. You'd like to pay by card.

b **Conversation 2.** You're a sales assistant at a store. Student A is your customer. You have four plates, and they are $3 each. Your customer can pay by card. Start a conversation with *Hello, can I help you?*

c ⋙ Now go back to p. 61.

10C STUDENT B

a **Conversation 1.** Read your first card. Think about what you want to say. Listen to Student A and reply.

1 You're a ticket agent at a train station.

- Time now: 11:15 a.m.
- Platform 6 is a two-minute walk.

	Time	Platform
Chicago	11:17 a.m.	6
Chicago	11:35 a.m.	6

b **Conversation 2.** Now read your second card. Think about what you want to say. Then start the conversation with Student A with *Excuse me.*

2 You want to go to Phoenix.

- Time now: 2:45 p.m.
- Ask about the next bus.
- Ask about the bus stop.
- Ask about the price. (You only have $15 with you.)

c ⋙ Now go back to p. 85.

7A STUDENT A

a You have a stall at a flea market. You sell the objects in the box.

cups glasses plates plants knives

Write a price for each object.

b Try to sell things to Student B.

It's only $5 – it's very cheap.

They're $3 each. They're very beautiful.

c At Student B's stall, you see three things you like:

- a beautiful old picture
- a lamp
- some interesting old books

Try to buy them for a good price.

It's very expensive. Is $10 OK?

8A STUDENT A

a Ask Student B about Morgan.

Where was she a year ago?

Where was she last weekend?

Was she at work on Monday?

b Listen to Students B and C talk about Marcella.

c Answer Student C's questions about Jaime.

1 year ago	last weekend	on Monday
in Chile	at a party in Medellín	at work in Bogotá

Jaime

d What is the same for all three people?

11C STUDENT A

a You and Student B live in the same city. Talk about good places for tourists to visit. This is what you think of the four main places to visit:

the Museum of History – very interesting
Central Park – OK, nice
Old Town – a little boring
Mega Department Store – very expensive

What do you think of Central Park?

I think Central Park is OK.

Really? I don't think so.

b Now go back to p. 93.

9B STUDENT B

a Ask Student A these questions about the weather in Mumbai, in India.

What was the weather like yesterday?

What's the weather like today?

What's the weather like in summer?

b Read the information about the weather in Berlin, in Germany. Listen to Student A and reply.

Weather in Berlin	
Yesterday	wet, windy
Today	sunny, cold
Winter	snows, cold

c Now go back to p. 75.

8B STUDENT A

a Look at the pictures of Leo's day yesterday. Write notes about what he did.

b Tell Student B what Leo did yesterday.

c Listen to Student B talk about what Charlotte did yesterday. What activities are the same?

7B STUDENT B

a Look at picture 2. Write notes about their clothes.

b Listen to Student A talk about the clothes in picture 1. Tell him/her the people's names.

c Tell Student A about the clothes the people in picture 2 are wearing. Find out their names and write them under each picture.

This person has a coat and pants. What's the person's name?

d Now go back to p. 58.

9A STUDENT A

a Read notes about your trip to Seville, in Spain. Make sentences from the notes. Use the simple past.

- in the south of Spain
- plane to Madrid …
- … then train to Seville
- small hotel – downtown
- a lot of photos
- shopping – didn't buy anything
- restaurants – very good food
- a concert – you liked it!

b Tell Student B about your trip.

c Listen to Student B talk about a trip to Dubai. Find four things you both did on your trips.

11C STUDENT B

a You and Student A live in the same city. Talk about good places for tourists to visit. This is what you think of the four main places to visit:

the Museum of History – OK
Central Park – boring
Old Town – beautiful
Mega Department Store – a lot of fun

What do you think of the Museum of History?

I think the museum is OK.

Really? I don't think so.

b Now go back to p. 93.

10B STUDENT A

a Look at the picture. What are the people doing? Write notes.

b Student B has a similar picture. Ask and answer questions to find five differences. You start. Ask about Ali.

Is Ali in the kitchen?

Yes, he is.

Is he eating?

No, he's not. He's …

c Now go back to p. 83.

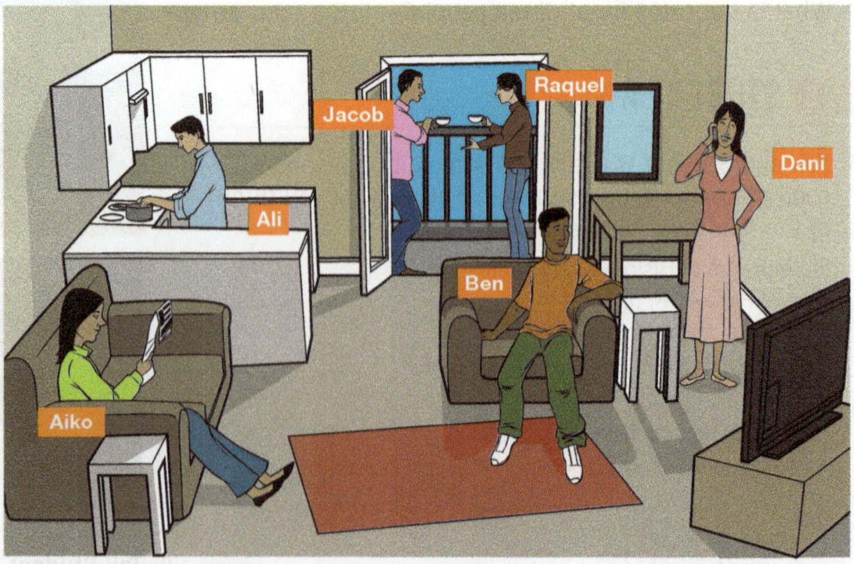

8A STUDENT C

a Listen to Students A and B talk about Morgan.

b Answer Student B's questions about Marcella.

1 year ago	last weekend	on Monday
in Canada	at a party in Orlando	in a meeting at work

c Ask Student A about Jaime.

Where was he a year ago?

Where was he last weekend?

Was he at work on Monday?

d What is the same for all three people?

12C STUDENT B

a You want to invite Student A to:

1 go out for dinner one evening.
2 go shopping for clothes.

Think about what you want to say. Listen to Student A and reply. Try to find times when you're both free.

Do you want to go out for dinner?

YOUR SCHEDULE

SUN	
MON	work 8:00–6:00 theater 8:00 p.m.
TUES	
WED	work 8:00–6:00 Spanish class 7:00–8:30
THURS	on vacation – not here
FRI	on vacation – not here
SAT	soccer 9:00–2:00

b Now go back to p. 101.

10A STUDENT A

a Carlos is in picture 2. Tell Student B:

- where he is (*He's sitting in …*)
- what's in the next room (*There's a … next door.*)
- what he's doing (*He's …*)

b Listen to Student B. Are they talking about picture 4, 5, or 6?

c Choose picture 4 or 5. Describe it to Student B.

d Listen to Student B again. Which picture are they talking about now?

GRAMMAR FOCUS

7A *this, that, these, those*

07.06

this, these = here, near me

"My brother wants ***this*** *car."*

"I love ***these*** *flowers."*

that, those = there, not near me

"My sister wants ***that*** *car."*

"I love ***those*** *flowers."*

Singular	***this*** *car*	***that*** *car*
Plural	***these*** *flowers*	***those*** *flowers*

***this/that/these/those* + be**

That's *my car.*
These are *your flowers.*
Those are *my books.*
Is this *your bag?*

***this/that/these/those* + noun**

I like ***that car****.*
These flowers *are beautiful.*
Those books *are big.*
This bag *is red.*

7B Possessive *'s*

07.17

Kristina's Zane**'s** sister. → Kristina is Zane**'s** sister.
Millie's Kristina**'s** friend. → Millie is Kristina**'s** friend.
KRISTINA My brother**'s** jeans are light blue. NOT ~~***The jeans of my brother*** *are light blue.*~~
The girls**'** dresses are beautiful.

Zane and Kristina**'s** parents are Lara and Jim.

Tip

We use **'** after the *-s* for plural nouns ending in *-s*.
→ *The* ***girls'*** *dresses are beautiful.* (2+ girls)

We use ***'s*** after a singular noun:
→ *The* ***girl's*** *dresses are beautiful.* (1 girl)

7A *this, that, these, those*

a Underline the correct words.

1 Excuse me, is *this / these* your coat?
2 Who's *this / that* man in the next room?
3 How much are *those / that* watches?
4 This *is / are* my wife, Tammy.
5 Are *this / these* your glasses?

b Complete the sentences with *this, that, these*, or *those*.

1 "Look at __________ beautiful house."

2 "__________ are our tickets."

3 "Who are __________ people?"

4 "Is __________ your phone?"

c Now go back to p. 57.

7B Possessive *'s*

a Complete the sentences with the words in parentheses.

1 It's Mara's skirt. (Mara / skirt)
2 It's __________. (Esteban / shirt)
3 It's __________. (Beth / dress)
4 They're __________. (Luke / jeans)
5 They're __________. (Sara / shoes)
6 It's __________. (Matthew / jacket)

b Write new sentences. Use the names in parentheses.

1 **His** new jeans are dark blue. (Sam)
Sam's new jeans are dark blue.
2 **His** house is near the train station. (Jacob)
3 **Her** shoes are brown. (Vanessa)
4 I like **her** new coat. (my friend)
5 **Their** new car is blue. (Rob and Emma)
6 **Her** new dress is pretty. (Penelope)
7 He's **his** best friend. (Ryan)
8 **Their** room is on the first floor. (the boys)

c Now go back to p. 59.

8A Simple past: *be*

Part 1: Affirmative

08.02

	+	
I/you/he/she/it	*I* ***was*** *You* ***were*** *He/She* ***was*** *It* ***was***	*in Seattle yesterday.* *in Los Angeles yesterday.* *in Houston yesterday.* *fun.*
we/you/they	*We* ***were*** *You* ***were*** *They* ***were***	*in Cartagena last weekend.* *in São Paulo last weekend.* *in Paris last weekend.*

She ***was*** *in Houston yesterday.* NOT ~~*She **is** in Houston yesterday.*~~
OR ~~*She **were** in Houston yesterday.*~~

Tip
We often use past forms of *be* with past time expressions like *yesterday, last night, two days ago, on Saturday, this morning.* (See Vocabulary Focus 8A on p. 149.)

Part 2: Negative and questions

08.08

	–	
I/you/he/she/it	*I* ***wasn't*** *You* ***weren't*** *He/She* ***wasn't*** *It* ***wasn't***	*in Seattle yesterday.* *in Los Angeles yesterday.* *in Houston yesterday.* *fun.*
we/you/they	*We* ***weren't*** *You* ***weren't*** *They* ***weren't***	*in Cartagena last weekend.* *in São Paulo last weekend.* *in Paris last weekend.*

I ***wasn't*** *at home yesterday.* NOT ~~*I'**m not** at home yesterday.*~~
OR ~~*I **not was** home yesterday.*~~

Tip
I ***was not*** *in Seattle yesterday.* → *I* ***wasn't*** *in Seattle yesterday.*
You ***were not*** *in Los Angeles yesterday.* → *You* ***weren't*** *in Los Angeles yesterday.*

08.09

***Yes/No* questions**		**Short answers**	
Were *you*	*in Los Angeles yesterday?*	*Yes, I* ***was.***	*No, I* ***wasn't.***
Was *she*	*in Houston yesterday?*	*Yes, she* ***was.***	*No, she* ***wasn't.***
Were *they*	*in Paris yesterday?*	*Yes, they* ***were.***	*No, they* ***weren't.***

08.10

***Wh-* questions**		
Where	***was*** *she*	*yesterday?*
When	***was***	*the meeting?*
Where	***were*** *you*	*yesterday?*
When	***were*** *they*	*in San Francisco?*

Where ***were you*** *yesterday?* NOT ~~*Where **you were** yesterday?*~~

8B Simple past: affirmative

08.15

Regular verbs	+	
talk	*I* ***talked***	*to her yesterday.*
play	*They* ***played***	*tennis on Saturday.*
like	*He was nice – I* ***liked***	*him.*
arrive	*They* ***arrived***	*last night.*

I ***talked*** *to her.* NOT ~~*I **was talk** to her.*~~

SPELLING: *-ed* endings

most verbs → add ***-ed***	*talk* → *talk**ed*** *play* → *play**ed***
verb ends in ***-e*** → add ***-d***	*like* → *like**d***

08.16

Irregular verbs	+	
go	*I* ***went***	*to a party on Friday.*
have	*We* ***had***	*sandwiches for lunch.*
see	*I* ***saw***	*Peter yesterday.*

I ***went*** *to a party.* NOT ~~*I **goed** to a party.*~~
We ***had*** *sandwiches.* NOT ~~*We **did** have sandwiches.*~~

See Irregular verbs on p. 103.

Tip
The simple past form is the same for all persons, e.g., *I played tennis., He played tennis., We played tennis.*, etc.

8A Simple past: *be*

Part 1: Affirmative

a Complete the sentences with *was* or *were*.

1. I ______ at home yesterday.
2. He ______ in the office in the morning, but not in the afternoon.
3. We ______ at the movies last night.
4. They ______ in Buenos Aires last month.
5. Two nights ago you ______ at your sister's house.
6. The movie ______ really great.
7. You ______ at school last week.
8. Ben and Jorge ______ at the basketball game on Saturday.
9. The concert ______ very good.
10. This morning I ______ at a café.

b Now go back to p. 65.

Part 2: Negative and questions

a Complete the text with *was, were, wasn't,* or *weren't.*

"It [1]______ Saturday yesterday, but I [2]______ at work all morning. I [3]______ (not) at my desk – I [4]______ in a meeting. It [5]______ very boring. In the afternoon, I [6]______ at home with a book – it [7]______ great. In the evening, my friend Michelle and I [8]______ at the movies, but the movie [9]______ (not) very good. We [10]______ tired, so I [11]______ (not) out late."

b Put the words in the correct order to make questions.

1. last night / were you / at the movies?
   Were you at the movies last night?
2. basketball game / was / on Saturday / he at the ?
3. were / the supermarket / they at / yesterday ?
4. you three / where were / years ago ?
5. interesting / movie / was the ?
6. China / you in / when were ?
7. was the / concert / where ?
8. a boring / was it / meeting ?

c Now go back to p. 65.

8B Simple past: affirmative

a Match verbs 1–6 with the past forms in the box.

arrived	had	watched	saw	stayed	went

1. go ______
2. have ______
3. stay ______
4. see ______
5. watch ______
6. arrive ______

b Underline the correct words.

1. She *goed / went* to Spain last week.
2. I *was sees / saw* my sister last weekend.
3. It wasn't a very interesting evening. Everyone *talkd / talked* about work.
4. I *staied / stayed* in a cheap hotel near the train station.
5. We *watch / watched* Germany vs. Uruguay last night.
6. She *read / readed* a magazine in the backyard.

c Complete the text with the past form of the verbs in the box.

have (x2)	go (x2)	stay	read	talk	watch	~~get~~

Last Saturday, Mr. Jones [1]___*got*___ up late, and he [2]______ a big breakfast. Then he [3]______ shopping. He [4]______ a pizza for lunch, and in the afternoon, he [5]______ to his mother on the phone for an hour. In the evening, he [6]______ at home, and he [7]______ baseball on TV. He [8]______ to bed at 10:30 and [9]______ a book until 11:00.

d Complete the sentences about you or your friends. Use the simple past.

1. Last weekend, ______.
2. Yesterday, ______.
3. This morning, ______.
4. Last Monday, ______.

e Now go back to p. 67.

9A Simple past: negative

She **didn't take** a taxi to the airport.

09.07

	–	
stay	*We **didn't stay***	*at a hostel.*
finish	*They **didn't finish***	*work early.*
see	*I **didn't see***	*them at the party.*
take	*She **didn't take***	*a taxi to the airport.*

*I **didn't see** them.* NOT ~~*I don't saw them.*~~
*We **didn't stay**.* NOT ~~*We didn't stayed.*~~

Tip

In the negative:
- add *didn't* before the verb
- the verb doesn't change

9B Simple past: questions

09.19

Yes/No questions		Short answers	
***Did** you*	***see** the movie?*	*Yes, I/we **did**.*	*No, I/we **didn't**.*
***Did** she*	***work** in a café?*	*Yes, she **did**.*	*No, she **didn't**.*
***Did** they*	***go** to the party?*	*Yes, they **did**.*	*No, they **didn't**.*

Did** you **work** … ?* NOT ~~Did** you **worked** … ?*~~
Did** she **go** … ?* NOT ~~Did** she **went** … ?*~~
*Yes, she **did**.* NOT ~~*Yes, she **worked**.*~~
*No, she **didn't**.* NOT ~~*No, she **didn't work**.*~~

09.20

Wh- questions		
Where	***did** you*	***work**?*
Where	***did** she*	***go**?*
When	***did** they*	***arrive**?*

*Where **did** you **work**?* NOT ~~*Where you **worked**?*~~
OR ~~*Where **did** you **worked**?*~~
*Where **did** she **go**?* NOT ~~*Where **did** she **went**?*~~

10A Present continuous: affirmative

We use the present continuous to talk about now.

10.07

	+
I	*I'**m writing** an email.*
you	*You'**re working** a lot.*
he/she	*He'**s**/She'**s studying**.*
it	*It'**s raining**.*
we	*We'**re watching** TV.*
they	*They'**re eating** a big dinner.*

*I'**m working** hard.* NOT ~~*I working hard.*~~ OR ~~*I'm work hard.*~~
*I'**m having** breakfast.* NOT ~~*I'm haveing breakfast.*~~
*I'**m sitting** in the car.* NOT ~~*I'm siting in the car.*~~

"It's raining and I'm writing this email ..."

Tip

*I'**m writing** an email.* → *I **am writing** an email.*
*We'**re watching** TV.* → *We **are watching** TV.*
*He'**s studying**.* → *He **is studying**.*

9A Simple past: negative

a Complete the sentences with the simple past negative form of the verbs in parentheses.

1 I didn't play baseball. (play)
2 I ________ early. (get up)
3 I ________ cereal for breakfast. (have)
4 I ________ my phone. (use)
5 I ________ my emails. (read)
6 I ________ a friend. (visit)
7 I ________ shopping. (go)
8 I ________ any photos. (take)
9 I ________ to the radio. (listen)

b Look at the pictures. Complete the sentences with the verbs in the box. Make one affirmative and one negative sentence.

arrive	play	go (x2)	have	~~get up~~

1 Last week, John didn't get up at 6:00. He got up at 7:00.

2 He ________ to work by bus. He ________ to work by train.

3 He ________ at work at 9:00. He ________ at work at 10:00.

4 He ________ pizza for lunch. He ________ spaghetti.

5 After work, he ________ baseball. He ________ tennis.

6 In the evening, he ________ to the movies. He ________ to a restaurant.

c Now go back to p. 73.

9B Simple past: questions

a Put the words in the correct order to make questions.

1 you go / where did / on vacation?
2 see / what did / you ?
3 you have / did / a good time ?
4 you / meet / who did ?
5 you / what did / eat ?
6 like it / you / did ?

b Complete the questions with *did* or *do/does*.

1 Where ________ you go last night?
2 ________ you see Jim yesterday?
3 What time ________ he go to work every day?
4 ________ they go to the movies every Saturday?
5 What ________ you do after class last week?
6 What time ________ their classes usually start?
7 What time ________ she start work yesterday?
8 Who ________ you see at the party last night?

c Complete the answers to the questions.

1 **A** Did you go home early?
B Yes, I did. I left at 4:00.
2 **A** Did they enjoy their vacation?
B No, ______ ______. It was boring.
3 **A** Did he watch the soccer game?
B No, ______ ______. He was at the movies.
4 **A** Did you go to the supermarket?
B Yes, ______ ______. We got some bread and cheese.
5 **A** Did your sister work in a restaurant?
B No, ______ ______. She worked in a café.

d Now go back to p. 75.

10A Present continuous: affirmative

a Write the *-ing* forms of the verbs.

1 eat ________
2 cook ________
3 talk ________
4 listen ________
5 get ________
6 have ________
7 wear ________
8 go ________

b Complete the sentences with the present continuous form of the verbs in parentheses.

1 I (wear) jeans and a T-shirt.
2 We (listen) to Drake's new song.
3 Lee (study) in her bedroom.
4 They (have) dinner at the moment.
5 Rob and Ben (play) soccer in the park.
6 He (watch) a movie in the living room.
7 Our children (cook) dinner for us.
8 I (write) this email at work.

c Now go back to p. 81.

10B Present continuous: negative and questions

10.15

	–
I	*I'm **not waiting** for the bus.*
you	*You're **not listening**!*
he/she	*She's **not reading** a book.*
it	*It's **not raining**.*
we	*We're **not staying** in a hostel.*
they	*They're **not working**.*

*She's **not reading**.* NOT ~~*She not reading.*~~ OR ~~*She's not read.*~~

10.16

Yes/No questions		Short answers	
***Are** you*	***waiting** for the bus?*	*Yes, I **am**.*	*No, **I'm not**.*
***Is** she*	***reading** a book?*	*Yes, she **is**.*	*No, she**'s not**.*
***Is** it*	***raining**?*	*Yes, it **is**.*	*No, it**'s not**.*
***Are** they*	***working**?*	*Yes, they **are**.*	*No, they**'re not**.*

***Are you** waiting?* NOT ~~*You waiting? You are waiting?*~~

10.17

	Wh- questions		
you	*What*	***are** you*	***doing**?*
he/she	*Where*	***is** he*	***going**?*
it	*Why*	***is** it*	***raining**?*
they	*What*	***are** they*	***watching**?*

*What **are you** doing?* NOT ~~*What you are doing?*~~

11A Object pronouns

Subject pronouns	Object pronouns	11.08
I	me	***I** talked to Mark last night. He called **me**.*
you	you	***You** were in town yesterday. I saw **you**.*
he	him	***He**'s a great singer. I like **him**.*
she	her	***She** lives nearby. I often visit **her**.*
it	it	*I live near Greenport. **It**'s a nice town. I like **it**.*
we	us	***We** were at the party. Did you see **us**?*
they	them	*These shoes are nice, but **they**'re expensive. I can't buy **them**.*

*He called **me**.* NOT ~~*He called I.*~~

Tip

We use *it* and *them* to talk about things and places.

***It** isn't a very interesting book. I don't want to finish **it**.*

NOT ~~***She** isn't an interesting book. I don't want to finish **her**.*~~

***It**'s a nice town. I like **it**.*

NOT ~~***He**'s a nice town. I like **him**.*~~

10B Present continuous: negative and questions

a Complete the sentences using the negative form of the present continuous.

1 She's not studying (study). She's watching TV.
2 They ____________ (have) lunch. They're having breakfast.
3 I ____________ (work). I'm at home.
4 He ____________ (play) baseball. He's watching the game.
5 We ____________ (stay) in a hotel. We're camping.
6 Are you OK? You ____________ (eat).

b Put the words in the correct order to make questions.

1 wearing / a coat / you / why / are ?
2 working / she / is ?
3 you / doing / are / what ?
4 are / where / going / you ?
5 she / is / texting / who ?
6 a computer game / playing / he / is ?

c Write two questions to ask your partner about now. Use the present continuous. Ask and answer your questions.

d Now go back to p. 83.

11A Object pronouns

a Underline the correct words.

1 We're waiting at the train station. Please come and meet *we* / *us*.
2 She was in town. We saw *her* / *him* there.
3 My parents live in London. I love to visit *them* / *they* on weekends.
4 I bought a pizza. Do you want to have *it* / *her* for dinner?
5 Where are my keys? Do you have *they* / *them* in your bag?
6 Here's a photo of my new boyfriend. I met *it* / *him* two months ago at a party.

b Complete the text with the words in the box.

he	she	it	we	me	him	her	us

JULIE THOMPSON, ACTOR
MY FAVORITE THINGS AND PEOPLE ...

1 My car
It's a very old Volkswagen, but I use [1]____________ every day.

2 My brother
[2]____________ works in Japan, so we don't see [3]____________ very often, but he always stays with [4]____________ on New Year's Eve.

3 The singer Lana del Rey
I think [5]____________'s a wonderful singer. I can listen to [6]____________ for hours.

4 My husband, Paul
We got married 30 years ago and [7]____________'re very happy. He always listens to [8]____________ when I have problems.

c Write sentences about your favorite things and people. Use pronouns in your sentences.

d Now go back to p. 89.

11B *can* for ability

> **Tip**
> *I **cannot** swim.* → *I **can't** swim.*
> For all persons (*I/you/he/she/it/we/they*), *can/can't* and the verb don't change.

Part 1: Affirmative and negative

We use *can* to talk about things we know how to do.

▶ 11.09

+	I/You/He/She/It/We/They	***can***	***swim.***
−		***can't***	***fly.***

*I **can swim** well.* NOT ~~*I can to swim well.*~~
*She **can swim** well.* NOT ~~*She cans swim well.*~~
*He **can't swim** well.* NOT ~~*He not can swim well.*~~

Part 2: Questions

▶ 11.14

Yes/No questions	+	−
***Can** you **swim**?*	*Yes, I **can**.*	*No, I **can't**.*
***Can** she **swim**?*	*Yes, she **can**.*	*No, she **can't**.*
***Can** they **swim**?*	*Yes, they **can**.*	*No, they **can't**.*

***Can you** swim?* NOT ~~*You can swim?*~~
*Yes, **I can**.* NOT ~~*Yes, I swim.*~~
*No, **I can't**.* NOT ~~*No, I not swim.*~~

12A *be going to*: affirmative and negative

Part 1: Affirmative

We use *be* + *going to* to talk about things we plan to do in the future.

▶ 12.02

	+		
I	*I'm*	***going to***	***get** some coffee.*
you/we/they	*You're*		***go** shopping.*
he/she/it	*She's*		***have** chicken tonight.*

*I'**m going to take** a bath.* NOT ~~*I going to take a bath.*~~
OR ~~*I'm going take a bath.*~~
OR ~~*I'm go to take a bath.*~~

Part 2: Negative

▶ 12.08

	−		
I	*I'm not*	***going to***	***go** on vacation.*
you/we/they	*You're not*		***read** a book.*
he/she/it	*She's not*		***visit** her sister.*

*We'**re not going to take** a bath.*
NOT ~~*We're going not to take a bath.*~~

12B *be going to*: questions

▶ 12.16

Yes/No questions			Short answers	
***Am** I*	***going to***	***see** you soon?*	*Yes, you **are**.*	*No, you'**re not**.*
***Are** you*		***go** out?*	*Yes, I **am**.*	*No, I'**m not**.*
***Is** he*		***leave** home?*	*Yes, he **is**.*	*No, he'**s not**.*

***Are you going to** … ?* NOT ~~*You are going to … ?*~~
*Yes, **I am**.* NOT ~~*Yes, I'm going.*~~

▶ 12.17

	Wh- questions			
I	*When*	***am** I*	***going to***	***see** you?*
you/we/they	*What*	***are** you*		***do**?*
he/she/it	*Where*	***is** he*		***live**?*

*What **are you going to** do?* NOT ~~*What you going to do?*~~
OR ~~*What you are going to do?*~~

11B *can* for ability

Part 1: Affirmative and negative

a Complete the sentences with *can* or *can't*.

1 I studied Spanish at college for three years. I ___________ speak with Spanish people.
2 Her meals are terrible. She ___________ cook!
3 My brother and I don't like the ocean or swimming pools. We ___________ swim.
4 I went to guitar lessons. Now I ___________ play some easy songs.
5 I don't have a bicycle, but I ___________ ride one.
6 I don't like that band. They ___________ sing.

b Now go to p. 91.

Part 2: Questions

a Put the words in the correct order to make questions.

1 you ride / can / a horse ?
2 well / cook / can he ?
3 sing and / can / play the guitar / they ?
4 can / draw pictures / she ?
5 speak / both Japanese / can you / and Mandarin ?
6 he drive / a car and / can / a bus ?

b Now go back to p. 91.

12A *be going to*: affirmative and negative

Part 1: Affirmative

a Complete the sentences with *going to* and the verb in parentheses.

1 I'm hungry. I'm ___________ (eat) a sandwich.
2 The house is dirty. He's ___________ (clean) it today.
3 We're bored. We're ___________ (watch) a movie.
4 It's very cold today. I'm ___________ (wear) a coat.
5 She's tired. She's ___________ (go) to bed.

b Now go back to p. 96.

Part 2: Negative

a Put the words in the correct order to make sentences.

1 his homework on / he's going / the weekend / to do
2 visit my parents / not / next week / we're / going to
3 going to / Friday night / I'm / party on / have a
4 they're not / to play soccer / going / on Saturday
5 not / cook dinner / she's / going to / this evening
6 to meet / tomorrow evening / we're going / some friends

b Complete the conversation with the correct form of *be going to* and the verb in parentheses.

A What are your plans for this evening?
B I [1]___________ (stay) home.
A That's not very interesting.
B Maybe not. But I [2]___________ (cook) a nice dinner.
A OK, and then maybe watch a movie?
B No, I [3]___________ (not / watch) a movie. I [4]___________ (read) a book. And you?
A Well, I [5]___________ (not / cook) dinner. I [6]___________ (get) a pizza and then I [7]___________ (go) to a party. Do you want to come?
B No, thanks. I [8]___________ (have) a quiet evening.

c Now go back to p. 97.

12B *be going to*: questions

a Make questions with *be going to*.

1 you / see / a movie / tonight?
Are you going to see a movie tonight?
2 what / you / do / this evening?
3 they / go / Italy / next summer?
4 when / you / have / lunch?
5 how / she / get to / the airport?
6 when / we / clean / the apartment?

b Complete the questions with *be going to* and the words in parentheses.

1 **A** ___________ home tonight? (you / stay)
B No, we're not. We're going to go out.
2 **A** What ___________? (she / buy)
B A new coat.
3 **A** ___________ shopping? (you / go)
B Yes, I am. Do you want to come with me?
4 **A** Who ___________? (they / invite)
B Oh, just a few friends. They don't want to have a big party.
5 **A** ___________ TV? (he / watch)
B No, he's not. He's going to work.

c Now go back to p. 99.

This page is intentionally left blank.

VOCABULARY FOCUS

7A Common objects 2

a 07.01 Listen and repeat the objects.

a bag (bags)

a chair (chairs)

a clock (clocks)

a cup (cups)

a glass (glasses)

a guitar (guitars)

a lamp (lamps)

a picture (pictures)

a plant (plants)

a plate (plates)

a soccer ball (soccer balls)

a speaker (speakers)

a suitcase (suitcases)

b Work in groups of three. Cover the pictures and make sentences. Add one more object each time.

At home, I have a guitar.

At home, I have a guitar and ten plates.

At home, I have a guitar, ten plates, and three big plants.

c Now go back to p. 56.

10B Place phrases with prepositions

a 10.08 Listen and repeat the phrases.

in the car

in a taxi

in a hotel

in bed

in/at a restaurant

in/at a café

at the subway station

at the airport

at the bus stop

at the movies

at a party

at home

at work

at school

on a bus

on a train

on a plane

on vacation

b Correct the phrases with prepositions.

1 It's 10:00, but he's still at the bed.
2 I'm waiting for the plane on the airport.
3 I can't talk now. I'm on the car. I'm driving home.
4 Are you in home or are you at the work?
5 I'm having coffee on a café.
6 John's not here. He's still in the vacation.

c Think about people you know. Where are they now?

I think my sister is on a plane.

My husband is at work.

d Now go back to p. 82.

7B Clothes and colors

a 07.13 Listen and repeat the clothes.

1

2

3

4

5
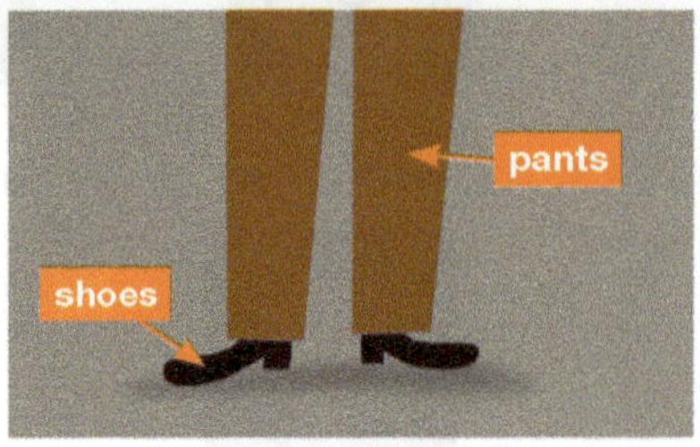

6

b 07.14 Listen and repeat the colors.

light blue | dark blue | light brown | dark brown | light green | dark green | light gray | dark gray | red | black | white | yellow

c What do the people usually wear? Write sentences.

1 Enrico usually wears a dark gray jacket and a light blue shirt.

2 ______________________

3 ______________________

4 ______________________

5 ______________________

6 ______________________

d Now go back to p. 59.

8A Past time expressions

a 08.03 Listen and repeat the days of the week.

b Complete the sentences.

1 Today is ____________.
2 Yesterday was ____________.
3 My favorite day is ____________, because ______________________________.

Tell a partner your answer in 3.

My favorite day is …

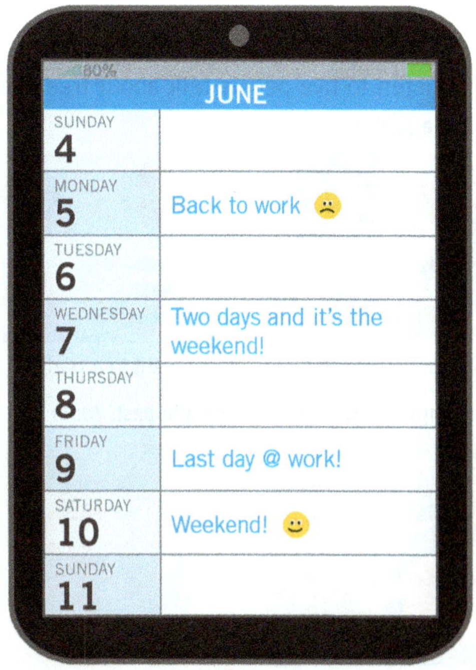

c 08.04 Listen and repeat the past time expressions.

yesterday

a year ago

last weekend

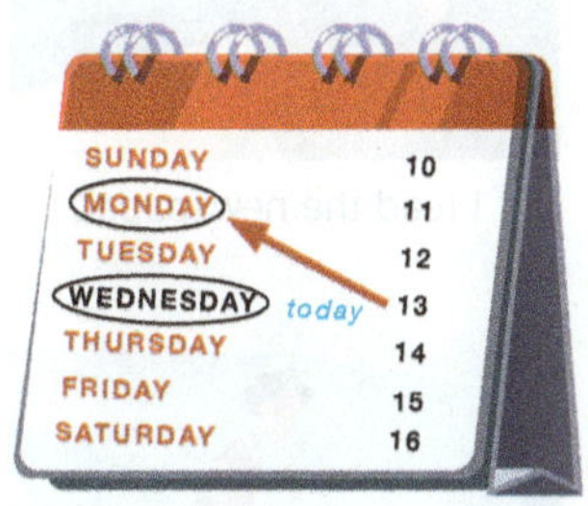

two days ago *or* on Monday

last night

this morning

d 08.05 Complete the chart with words in the box. Listen and check.

ago last on this

1 ______	night Sunday month weekend
a week two months ten years	2 ______
3 ______	morning afternoon
4 ______	Monday Friday

two months ago NOT ~~*before two months ago*~~
on Monday NOT ~~*at Monday*~~

e Complete the sentences with words from c and d.

1 I was in Barcelona ____________ weekend.
2 They were at the World Cup ____________ year ago.
3 Were you at home ____________ morning?
4 I was at a meeting two days ____________.
5 We were at work ____________ Friday.
6 He was at his friend's house ____________ night.

f Now go back to p. 65.

8B Free time activities

a 08.20 Listen to five people talk about free time activities. Put their activities in the correct order.

1 go (**simple past**: *went*)

☐ I went to the movies.

☐ I went to a party.

☐ I went shopping.

☐ I went to a café.

2 have (**simple past:** *had*); take (**simple past:** *took*)

☐ I had a pizza.

☐ I had a glass of water.

☐ I had coffee.

☐ I took a shower.

3 listen (**simple past:** *listened*); watch (**simple past:** *watched*)

☐ I listened to a podcast.

☐ I watched a soccer game.

☐ I listened to music.

☐ I watched a movie on TV.

4 read (**simple past:** *read* (/red/)

☐ I read a book.

☐ I read a magazine.

☐ I read the newspaper.

5 play (**simple past:** *played*)

☐ I played the guitar.

☐ I played a video game.

☐ I played soccer.

b 08.21 Listen and repeat the present and past verbs in a.

c Complete the sentences with the correct simple past verb.

1 We ____________ basketball on TV last night.
2 He had breakfast and ____________ the newspaper.
3 I ____________ to a party last night until 2:00.
4 I ____________ to music on the bus this morning.
5 We went to a café and ____________ a pizza.

d Write two true sentences about a free time activity in a.

On Friday, I went to a party.

e Read the first part of your sentences in d. Stop at the verb! Your partner guesses the second part of the sentence.

On Friday, I went ...

... to the movies ... ?

No, try again!

f Now go back to p. 67.

9A Transportation

a 09.02 Listen and repeat the words.

b Cover the transportation pictures in a. What do these signs show?

1 
2 
3 
4 
5 
6 
7 
8 

c Which kind of transportation do you prefer? Why?

d Notice how we use *go by* and *take* with different kinds of transportation.

go by	bus train plane tram

take	a bus a train a taxi a tram

go by bus NOT ~~*go with bus, go by the bus*~~
We can also use *take the bus, take the train,* or *take the tram.* NOT ~~*take the taxi*~~

e 09.03 Check (✓) the activity you see. Then listen and check.

1 
☐ I go to work by train.
☐ I drive to work.

2 
☐ He takes a taxi to school.
☐ He takes a bus to school.

3 
☐ She drives to work.
☐ She takes a tram to work.

4 
☐ She takes the subway to see her parents.
☐ She goes by plane to see her parents.

5 
☐ They always walk to school.
☐ They take the subway to school.

f Think of three places you went to in the last year. Write how you got there.

I drove to a friend's house yesterday.
I flew to Turkey last summer.

Tell a partner your sentences.

g Now go back to p. 72.

9B The seasons and the weather

a 09.12 Listen and repeat the seasons.

spring

summer

autumn/fall

winter

b Look at pictures 1–5 below. Which season do you think it is in each picture?

c 09.13 Complete the sentences with the words in the box. Listen and check.

windy sunny snowy rainy cloudy

1 It often **rains** in Vancouver. (verb)
There's a lot of **rain** in Vancouver. (noun)
It's often ____________ in Vancouver. (adjective)

2 It often **snows** in Antarctica. (verb)
There's always **snow** in Antarctica. (noun)
It's always ____________ in Antarctica. (adjective)

3 There's a lot of **wind** in my town. (noun)
It's often ____________ in my town. (adjective)

4 It's very **sunny** and **hot** today. (adjectives)
It was ____________ and **warm** yesterday. (adjectives)

5 There are a lot of **clouds** today. (noun)
It's ____________ and **cold** today. (adjectives)

d Underline the correct words.

1 Do you like hot and *sun / sunny* weather?
2 Is the weather *cloudy / cloud* today?
3 Is winter cold and *snow / snowy* in your country?
4 Is summer hot and *sunny / sun* in your country?
5 Does it *rainy / rain* in the fall in your country?

e Ask and answer the questions in d with a partner.

f Now go back to p. 75.

10A The home

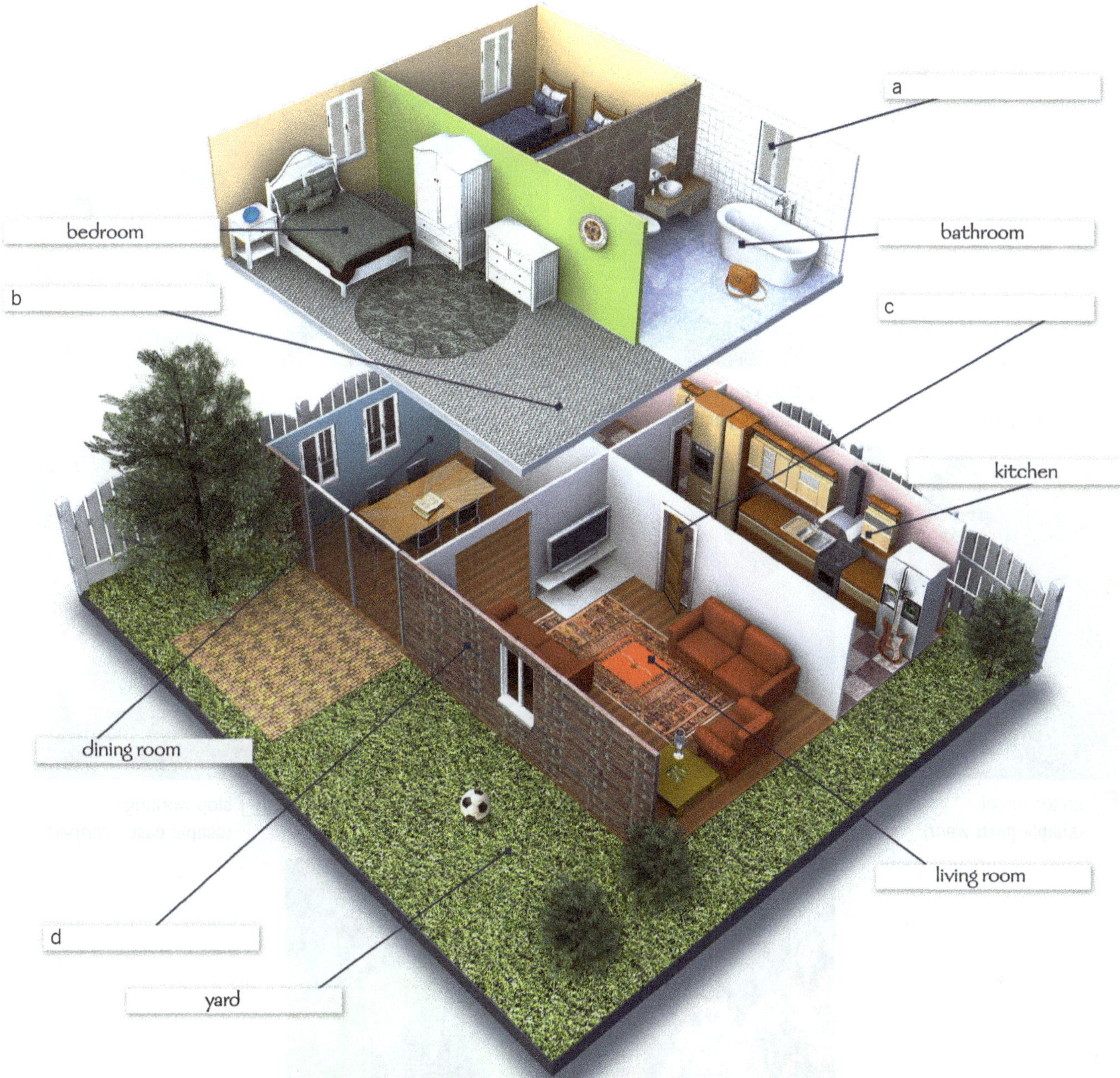

a Look at the picture. Where are objects 1–6? Ask and answer questions with a partner.

1 the glass	3 the book	5 the guitar
2 the bag	4 the soccer ball	6 the plate

Where's the glass?

It's in the living room.

b 10.02 Match the words in the box with a–d in the picture. Listen and check.

wall window floor door

c Complete the sentences with the correct words.

1 My family has dinner in the d____________ r____________ every evening.
2 We have a small y____________ behind our house. We often sit there on summer evenings.
3 My bedroom has a large w____________, and I can see the mountains.
4 I don't need a chair – I can sit on the f____________.
5 There are a lot of pictures on the w____________ in the dining room.
6 After dinner I like to read in the l____________ r____________.
7 My brother is always in the b____________ – he likes long showers.
8 There are two d____________s in the dining room – one goes to the kitchen, the other to the living room.

d Now go back to p. 80.

11A Life events

a Put the life events in the order you think is correct.

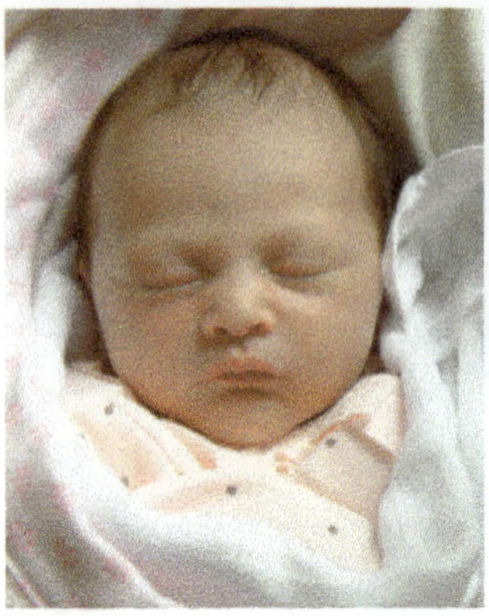

☐ be born
(**simple past:** *was born*)

☐ finish college
(**simple past:** *finished*)

☐ grow up
(**simple past:** *grew up*)

☐ get married
(**simple past:** *got*)

☐ go to school
(**simple past:** *went*)

☐ have a baby
(**simple past:** *had*)

☐ finish school
(**simple past:** *finished*)

☐ stop working
(**simple past:** *stopped*)

☐ go to college
(**simple past:** *went*)

☐ die
(**simple past:** *died*)

b 11.04 Listen and repeat the verb phrases in a.

c Complete the sentences with the verbs in parentheses.

1 I ____________ (go to) college when I was 18, and I ____________ (finish) college when I was 24.
2 Nelson Mandela ____________ (be born) in 1918, and he ____________ (die) in 2013.
3 My father ____________ (stop) working when he was 68.
4 She ____________ (get married) when she was 25, and she ____________ (have) a baby two years later.
5 I ____________ (finish) school when I was 16, and I ____________ (get) a job in a car factory.
6 Michelle Obama ____________ (be born) in 1964, and she ____________ (grow up) in Chicago.

d 11.05 Look at the answers and complete the questions. Listen and check.

1 **Q** ____________ go to school? **A** In New York.
2 **Q** ____________ finish? **A** In 2016.
3 **Q** ____________ do after that?
A I went to Canada.
4 **Q** ____________ go there?
A My brother lives there.
5 **Q** ____________ like it? **A** Yes, I had a great time.

e Ask and answer the questions in d with a partner. Say answers that are true for you.

f Now go back to p. 89.

11B Abilities

a 11.10 Listen and repeat the verbs.

swim
(**simple past:** *swam*)

cook
(**simple past:** *cooked*)

paint
(**simple past:** *painted*)

sing
(**simple past:** *sang*)

dance
(**simple past:** *danced*)

drive a car
(**simple past:** *drove*)

play volleyball

play cards

(**simple past:** *played*)

ride a horse

ride a bike

(**simple past:** *rode*)

run
(**simple past:** *ran*)

b 11.11 Complete the phrases with verbs in a. Listen and check.

1 ____________ a picture

2 ____________ a motorcycle

3 ____________ a song

4 ____________ dinner

5 ____________ basketball

6 ____________ to work

c Write four sentences about what you did:

- yesterday
- last night
- last weekend
- last Monday

Yesterday I drove my car to work.
I danced at a party last weekend.

Tell a partner your sentences.

Last night …

d Now go back to p. 91.

12A Months and future time expressions

a 12.03 Listen and repeat the months.

1 December, January, February
2 March, April, May
3 June, July, August
4 September, October, November

b Which seasons are 1–4 in a in your country?

c 12.04 Listen and repeat the time expressions.

tomorrow

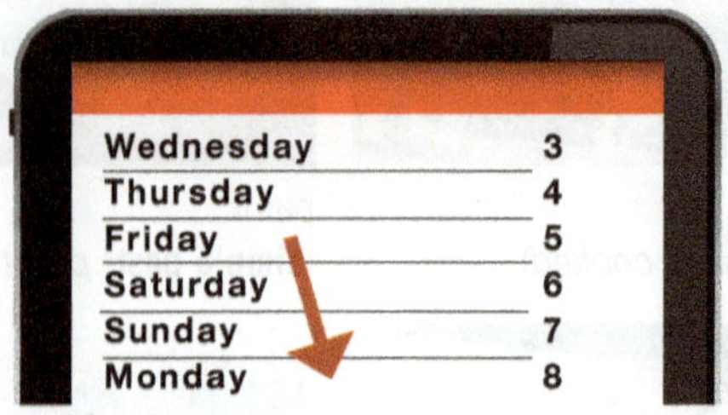

on Monday

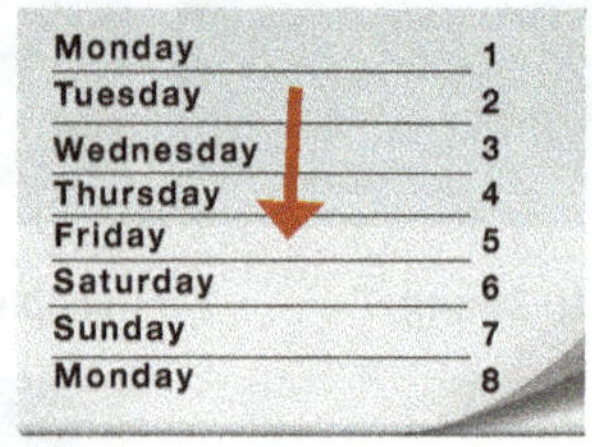

this Friday

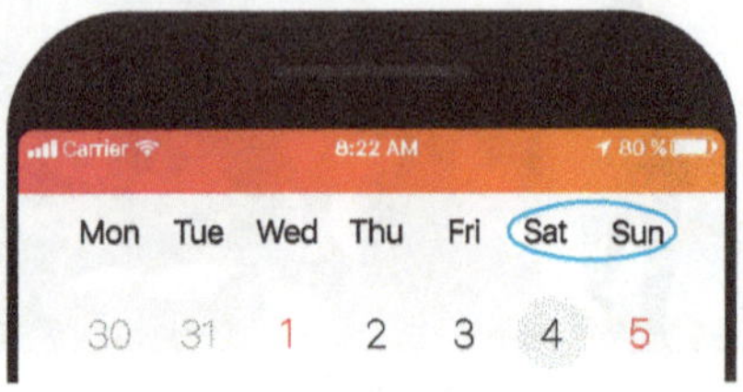

on the weekend

next Tuesday

in two weeks

d Complete groups 1–4 with words and phrases in the box. Some of them can go in more than one group.

Thursday	three months	June	winter	year	the winter

1 **on** Monday, Tuesday, Wednesday …
2 **this** afternoon, Monday, week, March, month, summer …
3 **in** March, the summer, two weeks …
4 **next** Monday, week, March, month, summer …

e Complete the sentences with a time expression.

1 I'm going to have (*meal*) ________________.
2 I'm going to go on vacation ________________.
3 I'm going to visit a friend ________________.
4 I'm going to buy a new (*object*) ________________.

Tell a partner your sentences.

I'm going to visit a friend tomorrow.

Ordinal numbers

a 12.05 Listen and repeat the ordinal numbers.

1 first, 2 second, 3 third, 4 fourth, 5 fifth, 6 sixth, 7 seventh, 8 eighth, 9 ninth, 10 tenth, 11 eleventh, 12 twelfth, 13 thirteenth, 14 fourteenth, 20 twentieth, 21 twenty-first, 22 twenty-second, 30 thirtieth, 31 thirty-first

b Work with a partner.
Student A: Say a number.
Student B: Say the ordinal number.

fifteen

fifteenth

c Now go back to p. 97.

12B Common verbs and collocations

a 12.11 Listen and repeat the phrases.

clean (**simple past:** *cleaned*) **exercise** (**simple past:** *exercised*) **go** (**simple past:** *went*)

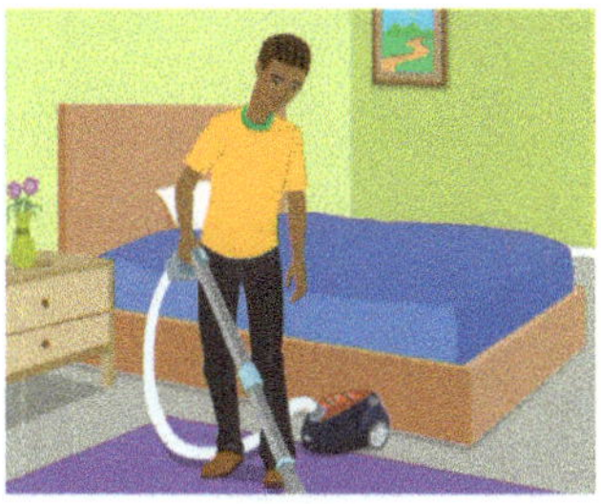
clean a room / your apartment

exercise at the gym

go to the beach

go to a museum

make (**simple past:** *made*) **play** (**simple past:** *played*) **visit** (**simple past:** *visited*)

make a cake

play sports

visit a friend

visit Paris

invite (**simple past:** *invited*) **use** (**simple past:** *used*)

invite someone to a party

invite someone for a meal

use a computer

use the Internet

do (**simple past:** *did*)

do yoga

do your homework

do laundry

b Underline the correct words.

1 He eats a lot and he never *plays* / *makes* sports.
2 It's my birthday next week. I'm going to *visit* / *invite* some friends to my apartment for dinner.
3 She's going to *paint* / *draw* the walls of her room dark green. Don't ask me why!
4 We were in Mexico and we *visited* / *went* Palenque.
5 I'm going to *do* / *make* some coffee.
6 A woman comes on Wednesday. She cleans and *does* / *makes* laundry for us.
7 Excuse me, can I *clean* / *use* your phone? I need to call my sister.

c Write three sentences with the phrases in a.

I'm going to clean my bedroom tomorrow.

Tell a partner your sentences.

d Now go back to p. 99.

This page is intentionally left blank.

WRITING PLUS

7C Commas, exclamation points, and question marks

a Look at the sentences and read about commas, exclamation points, and question marks.

Women's coats, blouses, jeans, bags – all in good condition. Not expensive!
How much are they?

, = comma ! = exclamation point ? = question mark

Commas

- We use commas in lists of nouns (things or people).
  Beautiful things for your home – ***chairs, lamps, small tables***
- We often finish a list with *and* + noun. We use a comma before *and* in lists.
  I'd like a bag, a coat, ***and a blouse****.*

Exclamation points

- We use exclamation points to mean *Look at this* or *This is important.*
  Not expensive!

Question marks

- We use question marks at the end of questions.
  How much are they?

b Add commas to each list.

1 For sale: old books newspapers magazines.
2 I love old cups plates and glasses.
3 She's wearing black pants a white shirt a gray jacket and black shoes.
4 They sell radios clocks pictures lamps tables chairs …
5 For sale: coats jackets hats shoes shirts dresses …
6 We need bread milk cheese and apples.

c Add a question mark (?) or an exclamation point (!) to each sentence.

1 How old are these things
2 Thank you
3 Write soon
4 New bookstore
5 Can I pay by credit card
6 How much are they

d Now go back to p. 61. Try to use commas, exclamation points, and question marks in your email.

8C Writing short emails, notes, and texts

a Look at the text and read about writing short emails, notes, and texts.

LOGAN

Hi Daniel!
Thank you for the tour of Newport yesterday. It was great to see a new town and meet your friends. I had a lot of fun! Here is a picture of all of us at lunch. I hope we can do it again some time soon.
See you soon!

1 We start **emails and notes** like this:
- *Dear* (name),
- *Hi* (name),

We are usually less formal in **texts**:
- *Hi* (name)*!*
- *Hey* (name).

2 In the main part, we use phrases like these:
- *I want to say …*
- *I was …*
- *Thanks for your email/note/text.*
- *It was …*
- *Thank you for …*
- *I hope …*
- *Here is/are …*

We often use the simple past, e.g., *I* ***had*** *a lot of fun. I* ***stayed*** *at home. I* ***went*** *into town.*

3 We finish **emails and notes** like this:
- *Best,* (name)
- *Thanks,* (name)
- *See you soon,* (name)

We don't usually finish a **text** with our name.
- *See you soon.*
- *Talk to you later!*

b Put a–e in the correct order to make a note.

a The food was great, and it was good to talk! I went home and watched a movie in the afternoon.
b I hope we can go to the concert on Friday.
c Hi Laura,
d See you soon,
Matt
e I want to say thank you very much for lunch yesterday.

c Complete the email with the words and phrases in the box.

hope	sorry	It was	Here are	Dear	talked

Reply Forward

1________ Allie,
2________ some photos of the party on Saturday night. I'm 3________ I was late!
4________ good to meet your friends. I
5________ to Emma and Marco – they're really nice!
I 6________ we can meet for coffee next week.
Best,
Janelle

d Now go back to p. 69.

9C Making the order clear

a Look at part of Sara's online post and read about making the order clear with *first, next, then.*

***First**, we went for a walk to the old part of the city.*
***Next**, we had lunch at a small restaurant.*
***Then**, we went shopping at a market, and I saw some beautiful things.*

When we write about events in the past, it's good to make the order clear. We use phrases like:

- *First, …*
  ***First**, we flew to Istanbul.*
- *Next, … Then, … After that, …*
  ***After that**, we took a bus to Claudia's town.*
  ***Then**, we went shopping.*

We usually use *Next* for the middle event, not the last event.
*First, we went to the zoo. **Next**, we had lunch. Then, we went shopping.*

b Underline the correct words.

The weather was very bad! [1] *Then, / First,* it rained. [2] *First, / Next,* it was very windy. [3] *Then, / After,* it snowed!

[4] *First, / Next,* we camped in Anton's backyard. [5] *First, / After that,* we stayed in a hotel.

Last summer I went to Canada with Veronica and Elijah. [6] *First, / Then,* we went to Toronto. It was great. [7] *Next, / First,* we went to Thunder Bay for three days. [8] *After this, / After that,* we stayed with Elijah's family in Vancouver.

c Add the words and phrases in parentheses in the correct place to make the order clear.

> We visited Emma's family in the country. We went to the city. (*then, first,*)
First, we visited Emma's family in the country. Then, we went to the city.

1 I went to a café. I went to the park. (*first, after that,*)
2 It was sunny and warm. It was sunny and cold. (*then, first,*)
3 We went to a restaurant. We saw a movie. We went home. (*next, first, then,*)
4 I finished work. I went for a walk by the river. I met her at the bus station. (*first, after that, next,*)

d Now go back to p. 77. Try to make the order clear in your online post.

10C Word order in questions

a Look at part of Anthony's message to Owen and read about word order in questions.

First, where can I find a taxi at the train station? And how much is it from the station to the hotel?

***Yes/No* questions**		
Do	they	have a yard?
Did	Eduardo	visit you?
Can	you	call me, please?
Is	she	working?

***Wh-* questions**			
How many rooms	does	your house	have?
Where	can	I	find a taxi?
When	did	the train	leave?
What	is	Selma	doing?

Questions with *be* are different.

Yes/No* questions with *be	
Is	Grace's apartment big?
Were	you at work today?

Wh-* questions with *be		
Where	was	your phone?
How much	is	it from the station to the hotel?

b Underline the correct words.

1 Where *are you / you are* going?
2 Who *is that / that is*?
3 *Did you use / You did use* your phone on the plane?
4 *You can / Can you* help me?
5 How many taxis *there were / were there*?
6 What movie *is your sister watching / is watching your sister*?
7 *There is / Is there* a yard?
8 How *you do often / often do you* watch TV?

c Put the words in the correct order to make questions. Add capital letters and question marks.

there / at the station / a café / is
Is there a café at the station?

1 where / the bus stop / is
2 do / when / start / work / you
3 you / the tickets / buy / did
4 some bread / you / buy / can
5 doing / what / you / are
6 the movie / is / what time

d Now go back to p. 85.

11C Pronouns

a Look at part of Leah's email to Hailey and read about subject and object pronouns.

... I study with a girl named Megan. She's from Ann Arbor ... She and her boyfriend Chris helped me a lot ... I often see them at the library ... I also know my brother, of course! ... It's good to have him in the same city.

We use subject and object pronouns so that we don't repeat nouns and names.

*I study with **a girl named Megan**. **She**'s from Ann Arbor and **she**'s really nice.*

*I also know **my brother**, of course! **He**'s really busy ...*

*I study with **a girl named Megan** ... She and **her boyfriend Chris** helped me a lot ... I often see **them** at the library.*

» Read more about pronouns in Grammar Focus 11A on p. 132.

We often use *you* to mean "people in general / everyone."
***You** can study English online.*

b Underline the correct words.

Seema Bhadoria is a young woman from India. People call [1]*she / her* "The Strong Woman." [2]*She / Her* can pull a truck with her teeth.
The Bajau Laut people can swim underwater for a long time. [3]*They / Them* are amazing humans. Did you read about [4]*they / them*?

William Higinbotham was a scientist. [5]*It / He* lived from 1910 to 1994. At a science lab, [6]*it / he* invented a machine called "Tennis for Two." [7]*It / You* could play tennis! [8]*It / He* was the first video game in the world, but he didn't make any money from [9]*it / them*.

c Switch the underlined words with the subject and object pronouns in the box.

he her him him it it me
us she she ~~they~~ they we

> I met a doctor and an IT worker. The doctor and the IT worker live in Madrid.
They live in Madrid.

1 Why is my sister eating that sandwich? My sister made that sandwich for me!
2 Do you like this picture of my wife and me? Valerie gave this picture to my wife and me.
3 My friends have a baby boy named Luke. My friends talk about the baby boy named Luke all the time!
4 Neil and Andy are students. Neil, Andy, and I met in college.
5 I'm Tony Smith, from school. Do you remember Tony Smith?
6 That's Ellie, and that's Jack. Jack likes Ellie, but Ellie doesn't like Jack!

d » Now go back to p. 93. Try to use pronouns in your email.

12C Paragraphs

a Look at Carlos's email to his friends and read about paragraphs.

Reply
Hi guys,
It's my birthday on Saturday. Do you want to come to my party? ← Paragraph 1 = invitation
It's at my apartment at 2:00. We're going to watch my favorite soccer team play on TV at 3:00. ← Paragraph 2 = making plans for the time and place
I hope to see you then!
Carlos

Paragraphs divide writing into groups of ideas. We use them to make our writing clear. In Carlos's email, he uses two paragraphs – one for the invitation and the other for making plans.
To start a new paragraph, write the next sentence on a new line, like this:

Reply
I'm sorry, I can't go. I have to work.

Do you want to meet on Tuesday?

Reply
~~I'm sorry, I can't go. I have to work. Do you want to meet on Tuesday?~~

b Match paragraphs a–b with 1–2.

Reply
1 ______
We could meet tomorrow. I'm free in the afternoon. What do you think?

Reply
There's a new restaurant in town. It looks really good.
2 ______

a Reply
Thanks for the lunch invitation, but I can't come today. I'm busy.

b Reply
Do you want to go there on Saturday?

c Rewrite the emails with two paragraphs.

1 Do you have any plans for the weekend? I'd like to see a movie. We could meet at the movie theater at 6:30. Is that OK with you?
2 It's my birthday next Friday. I'm going to be 25! Do you want to come here for dinner on Saturday? I'm going to invite a few friends.

d » Now go back to p. 101. Try to use paragraphs in your invitations.

Acknowledgments

The authors and publishers acknowledge the following sources of copyright material and are grateful for the permissions granted. While every effort has been made, it has not always been possible to identify the sources of all the material used, or to trace all copyright holders. If any omissions are brought to our notice, we will be happy to include the appropriate acknowledgments on reprinting and in the next update to the digital edition, as applicable.

Key:
U = Unit, CL = Classroom Language, C = Communication Plus, G = Grammar Focus, V = Vocabulary Focus

Photographs
All the photographs are sourced from Getty Images.
Front cover photography by Don Mason/Getty Images.
CL: Alexis84/iStock/Getty Images Plus; Witthaya Prasongsin/Moment; Eric Audras/PhotoAlto; Image Source; Farknot_Architect/iStock/Getty Images Plus; SDI Productions/E+; F. Lukasseck/Radius Images; **U7:** Cristina Arias/Cover; Danita Delimont; Dial-a-view/E+; Victor VIRGILE/Gamma-Rapho; Stefania D'Alessandro/WireImage; JP Yim/Getty Images Entertainment; Michael Loccisano/Getty Images Entertainment; Jamie McCarthy/WireImage; Aldomurillo/E+; Mint Images; Neustockimages/iStock/Getty Images Plus; Kettaphoto/iStock/Getty Images Plus; **U8:** FEBRUARY/Moment; Doble.d/Moment Open; Bay Area News/MediaNews Group; KeithBinns/E+; Tier Und Naturfotografie J und C Sohns/Photographer's Choice RF; UrosPoteko/iStock/Getty Images Plus; Mauriliers Schoenmaekers/500px; GK Hart/Vikki Hart/Photodisc; Andrew_Howe/E+; Geoff Scott-Simpson/Moment Open; Westend61; Mark Hunt; Pixelfit/E+; **U9:** Jeremy Maude/Photodisc; Nelsonarts/iStock/Getty Images Plus; Tatsiana Volskaya/Moment; StockstudioX/E+; GM Visuals/Royalty-free; Pigphoto/iStock/Getty Images Plus; Czekma13/iStock/Getty Images Plus; Allou/iStock/Getty Images Plus; J-wildman/Getty Images Plus; Jose Luis Pelaez Inc/DigitalVision; Simon Dux/iStock Editorial/Gett; Michael Lee/Moment; AntonioGuillem/iStock/Getty Images Plus; PRImageFactory/iStock/Getty Images Plus; Billnoll/E+; Danita Delimont; Floortje/E+; **U10:** Zero Creatives/Cultura; Cavan Images; KatarzynaBialasiewicz/iStock/Getty Images Plus; Gerenme/E+; Russwitherington1/iStock/Gett; Jacek Kadaj/Moment; John Keeble/Moment; JohnnyGreig/E+; Ppa5/iStock/Getty Images Plus; ExcellentPhoto/iStock/Getty Images Plus; FotoTravel/iStock/Getty Images Plus; Kohei Hara/DigitalVision; Flashpop/DigitalVision; PhotoAlto/Frederic Cirou; Luis Alvarez/DigitalVision; Jamie Squire/Getty Images Sport; David Madison/Photographer's Choice/Getty Images Plus; Baona/iStock/Getty Images Plus; **U11:** Sovfoto/Universal Images Group; Sven Creutzmann/Mambo Photo/Hulton Archive; Hill Street Studios/DigitalVision; Timothy Allen/Photolibrary/Getty Images Plus; OSTILL/iStock/Getty Images Plus; Kupicoo/E+; Vadimguzhva/iStock/Getty Images Plus; Artem Ermilov/iStock/Getty Images Plus; Hispanolistic/E+; Roy Mehta/The Image Bank/Getty Images Plus; Steve Cohen/Photolibrary; Greg Epperson/Photolibrary/Getty Images Plus; **U12:** Peter Cade/The Image Bank/Getty Images Plus; Westend61; DavidCallan/iStock; Simonkr/E+; Mint Images; AJ_Watt/E+; Cavan Images; Tim Kitchen/The Image Bank/Getty Images Plus; Synergee/E+; Wavebreakmedia/iStock/Getty Images Plus; Santypan/iStock/Getty Images Plus; Paul Bradbury/OJO Images; Vm/E+; Martin-dm/E+; **C:** Monkeybusinessimages/iStock; Vadimguzhva/iStock/Getty Images Plus; Ajr_images/iStock/Getty Images Plus; Adamkaz/iStock/Getty Images Plus; Juanmonino/E+; Drbimages/E+; Stevecoleimages/E+; Juanmonino/iStock/Getty Images Plus; Maskot; Leland Bobbe/Image Source; **G:** Eugenesergeev/iStock Editorial/Getty Images Plus; Chelsea Lauren/WireImage; **V:** Bravo1954/E+; Hyrma/iStock/Getty Images Plus; Sohel Parvez Haque/EyeEm; Devonyu/iStock/Getty Images Plus; Vofpalabra/iStock/Getty Images Plus; Eskymaks/iStock/Getty Images Plus; Guvendemir/iStock; MicroStockHub/iStock/Getty Images Plus; L_Mirror/iStock/Getty Images Plus; Carlosalvarez/E+; Steve@Colorado/E+; Christina Lease/Lonely Planet Images/Getty Images Plus; Judd Pilossof/Photolibrary/Getty Images Plus; Andrea Bricco/StockFood Creative/Getty Images Plus; Gbh007/iStock/Getty Images Plus; Twomeows/Moment Open; Ma-k/E+; Pjohnson1/E+; Seregam/iStock/Getty Images Plus; Subjug/iStock/Getty Images Plus; Juanmonino/E+; Animaflora/iStock/Getty Images Plus; Kirin_photo/E+; LindasPhotography/iStock/Getty Images Plus; Akepong Srichaichana/EyeEm; Chee Siong Teh/EyeEm; Ligorko/iStock/Getty Images Plus; Caziopeia/E+; Dimitris66/iStock/Getty Images Plus; Kutaytanir/E+; Hidesy/iStock/Getty Images Plus; Unpict/iStock/Getty Images Plus; RedHelga/iStock/Getty Images Plus; Bestfotostudio/iStock/Getty Images Plus; Gannet77/iStock/Getty Images Plus; Radionphoto/iStock/Getty Images Plus; Ariel Skelley/DigitalVision; Monty Rakusen/Cultura; Alvarez/E+; Monkeybusinessimages/iStock/Getty Images Plus; Image Source/DigitalVision; FatCamera/E+; PeopleImages/iStock/Getty Images Plus; Hoxton/Tom Merton; Wavebreakmedia/iStock/Getty Images Plus; Vav63/iStock/Getty Images Plus; Skrow/iStock/Getty Images Plus; Monticelllo/iStock/Getty Images Plus; Classen Rafael/EyeEm; Dan Thornberg/EyeEm; CostinT/E+; MortenBjerregaard/iStock/Getty Images Plus; Danielsbfoto/iStock/Getty Images Plus; Rosemary Calvert/The Image Bank/Getty Images Plus; Hudiemm/iStock/Getty Images Plus; Suradech14/iStock/Getty Images Plus; Golibtolibov/iStock/Getty Images Plus; Yevgen Romanenko/Moment; MDHayes/iStock/Getty Images Plus; John Seaton Callahan/Moment; Tramino/iStock; Oliver Strewe/Lonely Planet Images/Getty Images Plus; FotografiaBasica/iStock/Getty Images Plus; Marin Tomas/Moment; Rainer Grosskopf/Photolibrary/Getty Images Plus; John & Lisa Merrill/Photolibrary/Getty Images Plus; Jodie Wallis/Moment; Photographer Nick Measures/Moment; Fuse/Corbis; Real444/E+; IB/iStock/Getty Images Plus; Iliana Mestari/Moment; Vanessa Davies/Dorling Kindersley/Getty Images Plus; Skynesher/E+; Mark Williamson/Photodisc; Mlenny/Stock/Getty Images Plus; Prasit photo/Moment; Eli_asenova/E+; Quim Llenas/Getty Images Entertainment; PeTer_Lau; RUSS ROHDE/Cultura; Image Source; Shapecharge/E+; Lukasz Olek/Caiaimage; Jupiterimages/Stockbyte; UntitledImages/E+.

The following images are sourced from other Sourced/libraries.
U7: Alamy/LOOK Die Bildagentur der Fotografen GmbH; Bennyartist/Shutterstock; StudioSmart/Shutterstock; Raulin/Shutterstock; PodPad/Shutterstock; Ruslan Semichev/Shutterstock; **U11:** Emilio Segre Visual Archives/American Institute of Physics/Science Photo Library; Courtesy Brookhaven National Laboratory; CB2/ZOB/Wenn/Newscom; Sanjeev Gupta/EPA/Shutterstock.

Commissioned photography by Gareth Boden:U8

We are grateful to The Stephen Perse 6th Form College, Cambridge, for their help with the commissioned photography.

Illustrations
Illustrations by QBS Learning; Mark Bird; Mark Duffin; Sally Elford; John Goodwin (Eye Candy Illustration); Dusan Lakicevic (Beehive Illustration); Roger Penwill; Gavin Reece (New Division); Martin Sanders (Beehive Illustration); Sean 290 (KJA Artists); David Semple; Marie-Eve Tremblay (Colagene); Andrea Turvey (Eye Candy Illustration); Gary Venn (Lemonade Illustration).

Typeset by QBS Learning.

Audio by John Marshall Media.

Corpus
Development of this publication has made use of the Cambridge English Corpus(CEC). The CEC is a computer database of contemporary spoken and written English, which currently stands at over one billion words. It includes British English, American English and other varieties of English. It also includes the Cambridge Learner Corpus, developed in collaboration with the University of Cambridge ESOL Examinations. Cambridge University Press has built up the CEC to provide evidence about language use that helps us to produce better language teaching materials.

English Profile
This product is informed by English Vocabulary Profile, built as part of English Profile, a collaborative program designed to enhance the learning, teaching and assessment of English worldwide. Its main funding partners are Cambridge University Press and Cambridge Assessment English and its aim is to create a "profile" for English, linked to the Common European Framework of Reference for Languages (CEFR). English Profile outcomes, such as the English Vocabulary Profile, will provide detailed information about the language that learners can be expected to demonstrate at each CEFR level, offering a clear benchmark for learners' proficiency. For more information, please visit www.englishprofile.org.

CALD
The Cambridge Advanced Learner's Dictionary is the world's most widely used dictionary for learners of English. Including all the words and phrases that learners are likely to come across, it also has easy-to-understand definitions and example sentences to show how the word is used in context. The Cambridge Advanced Learner's Dictionary is available online at dictionary.cambridge.org.

CAMBRIDGE
UNIVERSITY PRESS & ASSESSMENT

Shaftesbury Road, Cambridge CB2 8EA, United Kingdom

One Liberty Plaza, 20th Floor, New York, NY 10006, USA

477 Williamstown Road, Port Melbourne, VIC 3207, Australia

314–321, 3rd Floor, Plot 3, Splendor Forum, Jasola District Centre, New Delhi – 110025, India

103 Penang Road, #05-06/07, Visioncrest Commercial, Singapore 238467

Cambridge University Press & Assessment is a department of the University of Cambridge.

We share the University's mission to contribute to society through the pursuit of education, learning and research at the highest international levels of excellence.

www.cambridge.org
Information on this title: www.cambridge.org/9781108862295

First published 2022
20 19 18 17 16 15 14 13 12 11 10 9 8 7 6 5

Printed in Great Britain by Ashford Colour Limited

A catalogue record for this publication is available from the British Library

ISBN 978-1-108-81813-1 Starter Student's Book with eBook
ISBN 978-1-108-81831-5 Starter Student's Book A with eBook
ISBN 978-1-108-81832-2 Starter Student's Book B with eBook
ISBN 978-1-108-86221-9 Starter Student's Book with Digital Pack
ISBN 978-1-108-86227-1 Starter Student's Book A with Digital Pack
ISBN 978-1-108-86229-5 Starter Student's Book B with Digital Pack
ISBN 978-1-108-81814-8 Starter Workbook with Answers
ISBN 978-1-108-81815-5 Starter Workbook A with Answers
ISBN 978-1-108-81819-3 Starter Workbook B with Answers
ISBN 978-1-108-81820-9 Starter Workbook without Answers
ISBN 978-1-108-81825-4 Starter Workbook A without Answers
ISBN 978-1-108-81826-1 Starter Workbook B without Answers
ISBN 978-1-108-81827-8 Starter Full Contact with eBook
ISBN 978-1-108-81828-5 Starter Full Contact A with eBook
ISBN 978-1-108-81829-2 Starter Full Contact B with eBook
ISBN 978-1-108-86223-3 Starter Full Contact with Digital Pack
ISBN 978-1-108-86224-0 Starter Full Contact A with Digital Pack
ISBN 978-1-108-86225-7 Starter Full Contact B with Digital Pack
ISBN 978-1-108-81833-9 Starter Teacher's Book with Digital Pack
ISBN 978-1-108-81810-0 Starter Presentation Plus

Additional resources for this publication at www.cambridge.org/americanempower